pedaling
PRAYERS
& perseverance

35 days
cycling solo
from Maine
to Key West

DAVID FREEZE

Published by:
Walnut Creek Farm Publishing
China Grove, NC 28023

Designed by Andy Mooney
Map illustration by Andy Mooney
Cover photography by Jon C. Lakey

ISBN 978-0-578-15199-1

Foreword

David Freeze has found a place for himself — on the seat of a bicycle.

One of my favorite scripture passages is in John's gospel, when Christ is comforting his disciples: "Do not let your hearts be troubled. You believe in God; believe also in me. My Father's house has many rooms; if that were not so, would I have told you that I am going there to prepare a place for you?"

I've always felt there is a "place" for each of us in our lives, a vocation or location where we can reach our fullest potential while also doing the most good. David Freeze has done many things in his 60 years, but he has certainly found a new calling — a new place — by tackling long bicycle trips and chronicling his journeys.

For two summers in a row now, he has left his North Carolina home behind to complete a challenging solo journey on his bike, first going west to east across the country in 2013 and then going north to south along the East Coast in 2014. As if pedaling up to 104 miles a day under the hot summer sun weren't feat enough, he found energy each evening to write about that day's sights and experiences. He would send this daily report and photos to the Salisbury Post, and the next morning Post readers eagerly opened their papers to see where David was now.

What David wrote for the paper was not the whole story, though. Sometimes his brushes with danger were scarier than he let on to the folks back home. And sometimes his encounters with people along the way were, well, more colorful than he wanted to describe in a family newspaper.

That's why this book and the one that preceded it make good reading, together or separately, even for people who read David's daily dispatches. At the end of the journey, David looks back and puts it all in perspective. The book definitely tells a fuller story.

It takes great faith for David to go on these quests — faith in himself, faith in his bike, faith in fellow travelers. And, above all, it takes faith in that greater power that propels and protects us each along this journey called life. God doesn't find us parking spaces or send down quiz answers — he may not even control a distracted driver pulling out of a parking lot, as David learned. But He's with us along the way and grants us the peace and confidence — and helping hands — to deal with what comes.

The titles of David's books sum up his attitude. The first was "Lord, Ride with Me Today." Now we have "Pedaling, Prayer and Perseverance." Each covers a pilgrimage of sorts, with David doggedly pedaling toward the ocean at the end of the trip and then getting home to his own piece of heaven on earth — his farm in rural Rowan County.

Along the way David encounters lots of people; his goal was to meet at least one a day. And he lifts lots of hearts as readers back home follow his travels. His trip is their trip.

The day before he left to start the Maine-to-Florida route, David stopped by the Post to pick up a light but thick envelope which a reader had dropped off for him. He later told me it had contained an angel made of yarn, perfect for taking along on the trip.

I had long forgotten that angel by the time the Post held a reception for David after the trip was complete. A woman walked up to him and simply said, "I'm Patsy." David's face lit up. She was the person who sent the angel, and she was happy to know David and the angel made it home in one piece, even if his bike did not.

I realized then that, while David may have traveled solo on this trip, he was far from alone. Countless prayers went with him. And there was at least one angel along for the ride.

— **Elizabeth Cook**
Editor, Salisbury Post

Acknowledgments

Just as in my previous book, "Lord, Ride with me Today," I owe the completion of "Pedaling, Prayers and Perseverance" to so many people who are more talented than I am. It has been a real honor to work with them. I find riding the bike for long distances much easier than to sit for endless hours putting this book together. Several skilled professionals have once again led the way toward the timely and quality completion of another book about one of my bicycle adventures. Again on the frontline were my friends from the Salisbury Post, our hometown newspaper. Editor Elizabeth Cook once again contributed to the book, and Jon C. Lakey provided his fantastic photography, always making me look better than I really do. Andy Mooney pulled it all together with his fine work on graphics, layout and design. It is easy to see why the Salisbury Post is one of the top newspapers in the Southeast. Chris Verner was the lead editor this time. Joe Ellis, accomplished author, runner, minister, teacher and more from Martin's Ferry, Ohio, gave me more insight on marketing and publishing the book. Cotton Ketchie, author, painter and photographer from Mooresville, N.C., weighed in and offered suggestions about what to see and best routes along the East Coast. While I was away, neighbor Ollie McKnight and nephew Sam Freeze took care of things on the farm. As always, my two daughters, Ashley and Amber, continue to be the daughters that make me prouder than I could have imagined. I love you both, and thank you for supporting me in these long-distance cycling adventures.

I am thankful to God for making sure I don't really have to ride solo. I don't worry; I just pray to Him and keep pedaling.

Introduction

I admit to being apprehensive at the start, but in June 2013, I left Astoria, Ore., heading east. My goal was the Atlantic Ocean surf of Myrtle Beach, S.C. More than 4,000 miles of solo cycling over the Rockies, through the heat of the Midwest and the ever-increasing traffic of the Carolinas became the greatest adventure of my life. At an average of 12 miles per hour, I saw parts of America that I had only dreamed of before.

The spectacular scenery of Oregon, Idaho, Wyoming and Montana was the backdrop as I tested my own limits, both physically and mentally. A special afternoon less than a week into the ride gave me the confidence that cycling across the country was something I could do. But best of all, it was something that was good for me in many ways.

Riding solo meant that when I made a wrong turn, I turned around and rode the extra miles to get back on track. When a tire went flat, I figured out why and fixed it. I carried my own tools and my own supplies, weighing the balance between how many pounds of water I could carry and still ascend mountains more than 11,000 feet high.

What began with me wondering whether I had what it takes to ride from coast to coast became a downright love affair with America and even more so with its people. I met some colorful characters and many more people who went out of their way to be helpful. People in Montana and Missouri had lots in common, the same as those in Kansas and Virginia. Good people still existed, and not once in 4,164 miles did I ever feel threatened. At the bike shop in Astoria, on the first morning of the ride, the mechanic talked me into taking along a 2½-pound bike lock. I never used it and honestly don't think it ever crossed my mind.

Just as important, the folks back home took an interest in my story and my daily updates in the Salisbury Post. I had no idea that they would like it, and I am still amazed at how those who followed the story retained so many of the details. We talked at civic clubs, Walmart, churches and the grocery store. Nearly every conversation ended with some version of the same question: "So, where are you going next?"

That question had been constantly running through my head, too, almost from the time that I dipped the front tire of my Surly Long Haul Trucker in the waves at Myrtle Beach. The cross-country ride had been fun, but it was also a life-changing journey in so many ways. I wanted that first ride to come to an end, but then I didn't want it to end. No doubt, I was hooked and would need more.

After plenty of study about a new route, I settled on the Maine to Key West ride. I wanted to experience a different part of America, admittedly one with more people but also plenty of scenery, history and more areas that I had never visited. The idea of traveling from the easternmost point of America to the southernmost point added extra zing. I knew that traffic would be a much bigger part of this ride, only I didn't know how much. Here is the story of that second ride. This time, I knew my equipment and my ability were proven, and I was ready to go. Another adventure was ready to begin.

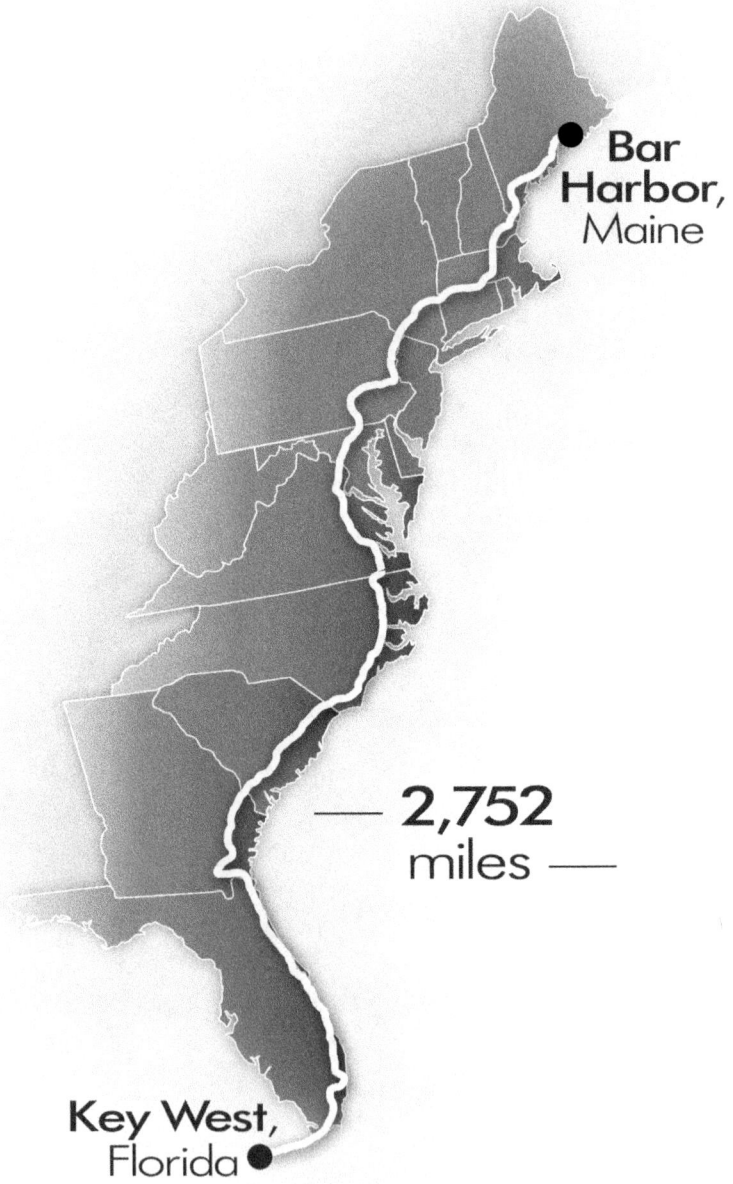

Bar
Harbor,
Maine

2,752
miles

Key West,
Florida

Chapter 1
— Ready for another ride —

How Maine to the Keys Came About

Early in August 2013, I finished my first long-distance bike ride. That sounds simple enough, but everything that followed was anything but simple. Coast to coast, Oregon to South Carolina, was 4,164 miles of a long-distance love affair with the back roads and people of America. It was the greatest adventure of my life, and I knew immediately that I wanted more.

Upon finishing the long ride through 12 states at Myrtle Beach, S.C., there was no doubt that my physical condition was not up to par. I was excited to be done, and ready to start running again. A day off relaxing on the beach was just the break I needed, or so I thought. There had been no rest days until I reached my farm near China Grove, N.C. Two days of riding on to the beach remained; however, I wanted to ride the busy roads filled with tourists on a weekend instead of a weekday when tourists and lots of trucks combine for major congestion. Those two off-the-bike days were filled with farm and yard work, washing clothes, maintenance on my Surly Long Haul Trucker, and lots of eating. I realized I felt tired, but I was still excited enough to plan for nearly 100 miles a day for the next two days.

While at home, I spent most of my time outside. As I worked near the barn and next to road, people stopped by to chat during both days. Nearly every cyclist who stopped wanted to hear what the ride had really been like. They wanted more information than I had provided in the newspaper updates. That seemed reasonable to me, so I vowed to provide more details in the upcoming book and in any future newspaper dispatches from another long-distance

1

ride.

I was surprised at some of the questions asked. Most of the cyclists said that they wanted to do something similar, and a few already had. One had gone on a cross-country ride with a large group. The most popular topic was the people encountered, followed closely in no particular order by weather, food, my bicycle and gear. The people in cars were more interested in hearing about where I spent the nights, how many showers I missed and how physically demanding the ride had been so far.

Early Saturday morning, I headed south from the farm, riding through the familiar towns of Faith, Rockwell, Gold Hill and Albemarle. While I had driven through these towns countless times before, this was my first time riding through on a bicycle. The perspective was so different. Things that mattered to a cyclist would never enter the mind of an automobile driver. Little things like curbing and drains, how much trash and debris was on the riding surface and especially how well the paving had held up all mattered greatly to me.

The temperature was rising, but I didn't care. Just before noon, I made an ice cream stop in Norwood that I sorely needed. Ice cream was my easiest source of a pick-me-up, and this one did the job. Just two more days of cycling, and I could take it easy and recover from the hardest physical challenge I had ever taken. Late that Saturday afternoon, I made it to the town of Bentonville, S.C., my planned halfway point. I had in mind that the only motel I had ever seen in the area would be fine for the night. I checked into the motel and then saw the room, by far the worst room on the whole trip. I couldn't stay there on my last night of the ride. After checking my iPad for another option, I went to the office and asked for my money back. Never before had this occurred on my cross-country ride.

After changing motels, I got a good night's sleep and headed for my last day of riding on this great adventure. What would the conclusion be like, I thought? Would there be much emotion when I neared the beach?

Through some of the heaviest traffic I had dealt with, I rode in the car lane without a bike shoulder for close to 50 miles. Car after car moved over and gave me room, though some of them kept the passing space to a minimum. Mid-afternoon, I spotted the Atlantic Ocean for the first time and felt my eyes watering with the realization that "Yes, I have done this! I made it!" The ceremonial wheel dipping of the front tire took place that afternoon, a moment of satisfaction like few I had known before. Friends had come to see and film it. This was certainly a grand day!

My daughter, Amber, had planned on coming down for the wheel dipping, but work kept her back in Charlotte. She was able to come the next day and bring my truck. She stayed only a few minutes and headed back home with a friend who had followed her to Myrtle Beach.

For the last few days, I had already been thinking that another ride would eventually happen. There would be plenty of time to plan it. Just finish this one, rest up a little, get my running legs back under me, and figure out what new states I wanted to see from my Brooks B-17 bicycle seat. Traveling this way was just too much fun for me to pass up another adventure.

My first sign that something might be wrong physically came just two mornings later. After that planned rest day on the beach, dozing and reading, answering messages from friends, and submitting my final update to the Salisbury Post, I couldn't wait to start running again. I went to bed, planning to go out the door about 6 a.m. for my first run in almost two months. Most of my running has been done in the morning over the years. I prefer to run before the sun comes up, getting a fantastic boost for the day. Traffic is usually lighter early in the morning, another solid reason for pre-dawn runs.

I have been a runner for 34 years, completing more than 72,000 miles by that August morning. Running usually came easy for me, even to the point of excelling in competition for many years. I was up at 5:30 a.m. and out the door by 6, excited to regain what I saw as my identity. Back home, people knew me as "the runner," a fact that has always been just fine with me. I had been waiting for weeks to go for a run with no responsibilities. Hoping for just three miles, I headed off down the sidewalk. But only a few blocks into the run, I had to stop to catch my breath. Nothing about that seemed right, but certainly I had never ridden for 54 consecutive days before, so I had no comparison to know just how that experience had affected my body. Even though my pace was slow, I felt as if I were pulling a sled.

After repeated stops, it was quickly apparent that this was not going to be one of my favorite and memorable runs as I had hoped. My breath was rapid, and I sensed that my pulse was too. When the run was over, my body felt drained of energy. I already knew that one of my ears seemed clogged, but that wasn't a big worry. Maybe I just needed to rest, I thought. The next morning's run, now back at home, was not much better.

For a few days, I kept expecting an improvement that never came. Always an optimist, I tied up my shoes daily and went out the door on what I expected to be a breakthrough run. After several visits to the doctor's office and increasing struggles to breathe, I was at a loss for what was happening to my usually reliable body. Theories to this point had been asthma or a heart condition that had developed from the stress of the long ride, much of it through elevation and extremely warm conditions. Tests proved neither the asthma nor heart to be the problem. Still, nothing was the obvious culprit. I kept trying each day to get back to normal.

The final straw came on an early morning run with a client. We planned to run only 3.1 miles, a distance that should have been easy for me. Yet, I felt out of breath and faint even before we made the first mile. The client was willing to walk with me back to our starting point, probably worried that something might happen if I were left alone. I knew then that I had to get to the bottom of this. My right calf started to hurt, and my breathing worsened. While doing some research on my own, I realized that the symptoms matched a possible deep vein thrombosis or blood clot. This information was in several sources online, one of them an endurance cycling blog. I read until bedtime and then got ready to go to sleep. By this time my breathing was so labored that I honestly was afraid I might not make it until morning. Instead of going to bed, I started to watch a movie. My fear was that I would fall asleep and not wake up.

I was waiting when the doctor's office opened. I told the staff that I might have a blood clot, and they looked amused. Without a doubt, I had a challenge in convincing my doctor that this could be the answer, even though he relented and sent me to our local hospital for testing. The doctor said, "There is no way that you have a blood clot. Healthy people don't have blood clots!" I was confident that I had the answer and wanted desperately to be right. If so, we could begin treatment, and life could soon return to normal.

Just 20 seconds into the test, a seven-inch-long clot was found in my right leg. We had the answer, but little did I know that there was much more yet to be found. The hospital staff quickly contacted the doctor, and the simple answer then became extremely complicated.

More testing that day found that at least four clots had lodged in my lungs, any one of which could have caused a blockage in my heart. I was immediately given a shot to help improve my blood flow and started on a blood thinner. No more running for a while, a fact that even I didn't argue with. Further testing found that I had an ear infection that soon responded to treatment with antibiotics and slowly began to improve. Two days later, I passed the first of two kidney stones within three weeks of the end of the ride. My urologist suspected dehydration as the culprit. Eventually, the doctors found that dehydration also played a factor in the formulation of the major blood clot. The elevation experienced while climbing through the Rockies, Cascades and other mountain ranges also contributed. I felt as if the perfect storm had come together to cause all of these problems in such a short time.

We were not done. Doctors wanted to make sure I didn't have any clots in the brain as well, so an MRI was scheduled for early the next Sunday morning. With my daughters in attendance, that testing uncovered a small brain tumor. My initial positive thoughts that morning included the fact that at least the tumor had been found early, and it appeared to be operable. By then, I couldn't believe the extent of the issues uncovered so quickly. No one could tell for sure how long the brain tumor had been growing. One idea was that it could have been there for years, consistent with the fact that my only previous brain MRI had been done at least 10 years before.

My visit to a brain surgeon was the most humbling experience. Patients and staff in the office were so pleasant and upbeat as we talked, while I wondered quietly how bad the other patients' individual situations were. The surgeon told me, as well as with my daughter, Amber, that we shouldn't worry. He felt that he could remove the tumor, and he doubted that it was malignant, based on its location and appearance. But, and it was a big but, he didn't want to operate as long as I was on the blood thinner. The surgeon told us that we should come back in six months for further testing.

The more I thought about it, the more certain I became that I wanted another opinion on the six-month wait. My doctors agreed, and I went to Winston-Salem to get that second opinion. That doctor immediately ordered another MRI, now almost two months since the tumor was found. With that news, I headed back to Salisbury to get the next MRI, ready for anything. Just a few days later, one of the most amazing things happened, with a result that would immediately affect the timing of my next bike ride.

Late on a weekday afternoon, I settled back into the MRI machine, listening to music just as before. Boldly I prayed for a good outcome, again just as I had before. The testing took longer this time, which had something to do with a slightly different MRI test being ordered. Eventually one of the attendants to the MRI machine told me that the doctors wanted me to relax and just stay where I was. She said, "There are two radiologists here now, and they may want to do some more testing." About 10 minutes later, she came back and told me to get dressed, but to wait there for one of the doctors to talk with me. My worry at that point was growing, thinking that the tumor might have gotten worse. Another 10 minutes passed before the doctor came in. I will never forget his first words: "What are you doing this afternoon?" My worry meter shot up even more, and I said, "I had planned on a little work around the farm, but tell me what you have found." I thought he might tell me that surgery was imminent.

My assessment was totally wrong, which soon became very apparent. The doctor showed me the images of the tumor from previous testing, and then showed me new images of that same area. There was no tumor in them, nothing at all that appeared out of the ordinary. We looked at the area from different angles, and all the images agreed that the tumor was gone. With that, the doctor said, "We have no explanation."

I smiled and thought to myself that this is exactly what all the prayers, both mine and those of many others, had requested. I will always be convinced that once again the power of prayer had been demonstrated in such a wonderful way. Within seconds I thought, "Yes, I will go on another ride, and I will celebrate this result." That evening, I went home and looked at a possible route from Maine to the Florida Keys. With great praise, I felt there was a greater plan than just my reasons for heading out on another adventure. Possibly those reasons included things that I would never understand, but regardless, the next ride was on!

Chapter 2
— Preparation and outlook —

Making my way to Maine

Now that the ride from Maine to Key West was going to happen, there was much to do. I had to get the bike checked out, get my gear together, order the Adventure Cycling maps, and spend some serious time planning the exact route and time frame. This ride would require a flight to Maine and a flight home from Key West, two out-of-the-way areas. My schedule was busy, and some adjustments would be necessary. I set out to get all of these things ready.

My Surly bike had not been ridden much since last August, especially with the medical issues requiring the blood thinner. The oncology doctor allowed me to run but asked me to stay off the bike since the blood thinner would increase the risk of excessive bleeding in a bicycle accident. I dusted the bike off and wiped it down, then took it to Salisbury and Skinny Wheels Bike Shop to have it checked out. There had been no issues with the bike last August at the completion of that ride, but now we had to plan for more than 3,500 additional miles. They found the bike to be nearly ready to go, needing only a new chain and a rear tire, not much considering all the climbing done last year crossing several mountain ranges. After those repairs, I brought the bike home for a few training rides.

Last year, I rode more than 40 miles several times to train for the long days on the bike saddle and had multiple 60-plus-mile rides in the past year. These long adventure rides are hard to train for, especially without loading 40 pounds of weight on the bike. Pedaling the bike is much harder with the extra weight on it, especially up the hills. I did not take the time during training to significantly load the bike. My running training had been going very well, and I hoped that the strength gained from it would help power the bike up the significant hills. Other cyclists told me that I should drop my running miles and spend more time on the bike, but that just didn't seem natural to me. As I have said often, I am a runner and not a serious cyclist. My long-distance training would come with two 100-mile days on the first two rides of the trip. Recovery would be the key, and I knew that my body had always been good at that. On the cross-country ride, it was commonplace for me to go to sleep feeling very tired and wake up in the morning refreshed and ready for more. I often went to sleep thinking of taking a rest day and then completely forgot about it when I woke up.

It didn't take long either to gather my gear. I was extremely happy with my tent and sleeping bag, though I wondered if the sleeping bag might be too heavy for this trip. It is rated to 40 degrees, about right for a few early summer northern Maine nights but too much for summer nights in the South. I briefly considered a lighter sleeping bag and later wished I had purchased one. I decided to take both the tent and sleeping bag as the mainstays of my plans to camp often, especially if the weather stayed moderate and motel rates were as high as expected. For at least three quarters of this ride, I would be cycling through areas in their peak season for tourism. Coastal areas often would be even more expensive, making me think that there would be plenty of camping in my near future. A very basic half-body air mattress and a small emergency flashlight closed out the camping gear. My pillow would be the sleeping bag's protective cover, into which I would stuff my available extra clothing and then pull the drawstring tight.

My same tool bag and emergency hand pump had done well the previous year, so I found no reason to change them. The hand pump was very small and required lots of pumping to fill up a tire. I planned to rely on the CO_2 cartridges for filling tires anyway. Two tire tubes and those CO_2 cartridges completed the tire supplies.

My complete clothing list included a pair of bike shorts, a couple of Dri-FIT short-sleeve shirts, one Dri-FIT long-sleeve shirt, a long-sleeve wool shirt, a light hooded Tyvek raincoat, two pairs of underwear, a pair of Dri-FIT shorts with a liner, and three pairs of Dri-FIT socks. All of these were lightweight items and would be very serviceable without taking up a lot of space. I planned to wear a bright pair of running shoes and use a red bicycle helmet with a mirror. People always wonder why I don't have more clothes and a second pair of bike shorts. I have learned from experienced long-distance riders to wear things a couple of days if need be. A good thing about the bike shorts and Dri-FIT T-shirts is that they are all easy to wash in the shower or sink, and they dry fairly well over-night. And if they didn't dry completely, wearing something cool and damp was not a bad thing on some of the steamy mornings. Drying would be enhanced once the breeze started as I pedaled down the road.

With these items all complete and packed in my Ortlieb panniers (saddlebags), I turned to some of the more complex issues. I didn't want to spend a fortune to reach Bar Harbor or to return from Key West, but all the flights seemed very pricey. With the help of Allison Tuck, my favorite travel agent, we got a great deal making the flights as part of a round-trip package. I had no idea this was possible, but Allison knew exactly how to pull it off. As she cautioned me, the only real issue was that I had to make it to Key West by August 6 and be prepared to fly out very early on the morning of August 7. Otherwise, a new ticket would be very costly.

I had previously met with Cotton Ketchie, well-known photographer, author and artist from Mooresville, N.C. Cotton knows quite a bit about the Eastern Seaboard, especially Maine and the rest of the Northeast. Cotton was excited that I would be spending a large part of my summer cycling from Maine to Florida, more so if I was willing to add on a little mileage to officially start the ride near Lubec at the easternmost point of the United States. He gave me plenty of maps, one for every state I might visit. Cotton's photography made me even more excited about spending a lot of time riding in Maine along the coastline. I knew that I wanted to see several of the lighthouses that were captured so well in his work.

My Adventure Cycling maps had arrived also, and with all of Cotton's maps beside them, I started in Bar Harbor and figured out a basic plan for the beginning of the ride. After landing in Bar Harbor, I would spend the night and then immediately head north for about 100 miles to Quoddy Head State Park, home of the granite monument that signifies the easternmost point. That idea was now going to be one of the themes of my ride. I briefly looked through the first five states, searching for any real issues if I followed the Adventure Cycling route. None stood out, and I didn't worry much about those things ahead of time anyway. There would be plenty of time to decide the exact route during my evening meals and on the road during the day.

A lesson learned on the cross-country ride was that specific planning for more than a day ahead was often time wasted. Factors like weather, mechanical issues, challenging terrain and ability to find supplies, motels or camping could quickly wipe out any well-laid plans that included specific times or dates to be in certain locations. I usually had a good idea of how far to ride on a given day, but often I would feel better than expected when I entered the last town. Sometimes the miles just went faster than I had hoped, and the opportunity arose to add another hour or two of riding. On a few occasions, I decided to take an afternoon break when I found something interesting to see that was not in the original plan. One of the few things that worried me is that no one knew where I was for most of the time on the long ride, but then again a certain level of excitement and adventure was the result of this.

With all those major issues complete, I had little to worry about. My running had made me feel strong and fit overall. My confidence level was high and I was ready to go. Skinny Wheels shipped my bike to a Bar Harbor cycle shop, and I sent my gear to the motel I had booked for the first night. That motel was very accommodating and the price was right, but only for the first night. Another night, made possible by the ride to Lubec and then the resulting return to the same area, would be much more expensive. I almost booked the second night but waited to see what would develop and whether I could handle the two long 100-mile days that would kick off the journey.

With less than a week to go before departure, I lined up my nephew, Sammy, to check on the farm each day. My neighbor, Ollie McKnight, would get the mail and also keep an eye on the place. My daughter, Ashley, was going to pay the bills, and my daughter, Amber, was set to take me to the airport. Not much happens at the farm during the summer, unless there is enough rain and cool temperatures to make the hay produce an extra cutting. To reduce this possibility, I made sure that we got in a good crop of hay just before my planned departure date. It didn't hurt to have a little extra money in the bank from hay sales because the unknown for this trip centered on the price of motel rooms.

On the morning of June 31, I flew out of Greensboro with connecting flights to Philadelphia and Boston before arriving in Bar Harbor. As I sat in the window seat on the first flight, I had a moment of apprehension about embarking on another major journey that once again had so much uncertainty. Early that morning, I made my first specific prayer of the trip, asking for safety throughout the journey. Several friends had been to Maine, and I had read quite a bit about the good and bad of the state. I expected from one source or another bad roads, huge mosquitoes, some very lonely areas and lots of climbing. I also expected friendly people who could help out with some of these things. After saying that initial prayer, I felt exceptional peace during the rest of the flying time.

The flights all went well, and soon I had my first glimpse of Maine. The heavily wooded areas near the ocean reminded me of the first sight of Oregon, the departure point for last summer's ride.

I caught the free Bar Harbor shuttle provided by L.L. Bean and eventually was dropped off at the Edenbrook Motel, the first of many on this trip. My gear was waiting for me, already in my room. So far, so good! Now to go find my bike. This part of the trip was exactly opposite of my travel day to Oregon the previous summer. On that day, the first flight was canceled, and several connecting flights got me to Portland way later than expected. The only way to make it to Astoria was by private shuttle, and I chose the shuttle over losing a day. I hoped that this year's better-than-expected travel day would signify a good start.

It was a short walk to the downtown area and the Acadia Bike Shop. I had to ask directions twice to find the place but finally walked in triumphantly, only to find my first problem. My bike was still in the box, and I was told they would not have time to assemble it that afternoon—all this after the bike had been at the shop for three full days. I found the owner and expressed my displeasure, reminding him of his promise to have the bike ready when I arrived. In the proper about-face, he asked that I give them an hour, and the bike would be ready. An hour's delay was better than an extra day, so I took the owner at his word. The other bike shop in town was much bigger and busier and made me think that I had chosen the wrong one. Still, I left the shop hoping that I would return to an assembled Surly that was ready to roll for about 35 days.

This delay gave me a chance to walk down to the harbor and look around the picturesque town, or village, as the locals called it. I loved the whole area and hoped that Bar Harbor was just the first of many historic coastal towns similar to it. With still some time to kill, I walked back to the Rexall Drug Store and ordered blackberry ice cream at the old-fashioned fountain. The ice cream was better than the look on the clerk's face when she had to fix an order for me at near closing time. She actually looked at the clock and frowned before she finally picked up the ice cream scoop. I smiled and ate my ice cream as I headed back to the bike shop. Harry at Acadia had my Surly ready to go. After having spent some time in bike shops, I knew he could easily get the bike ready to go. The seat and everything else looked correct and now it felt as if the adventure was going to be OK. I bought a few small items and pushed the bike down the street, making a couple of stops for some food—one for a slice of pizza and another for some snacks at a convenience store.

As the sun was setting, I headed back to the motel and loaded my bike. Tomorrow was going to be a big day and I needed to get to bed, but a problem with my cyclometer caused a delay. Cyclometers are bicycle odometers with brains. It took quite a bit of working with it to make the numbers look right and in the correct language. I guessed at the proper wheel size and hoped that the distance would then measure correctly. I took time to correctly load the bike with everything except for the few items I would need in the morning. Once I had the cyclometer working and the bike loaded, I went to bed with dreams of a successful start on my newest adventure.

I wondered whether the Maine roads would be as rough and the terrain as hilly as I expected. All of that was part of tomorrow's challenge. I needed a night of sound sleep, and then it would be time to go have some fun.

Chapter 3
— Maine —

Reaching the Easternmost Point
of the United States

I finally fell asleep on Monday night, worrying too much that I had forgotten something or that I was not ready for two back-to-back 100-mile days. Just being in Bar Harbor at the launching point of my journey had added to my excitement and a little bit to the butterflies. Even the historic little town was hilly, and it sits right on the water. Worry aside, I was wide awake about 5 a.m. and amazed that the eastern sky was already bright. It was time to get rolling! One of my purposes for making these long-distance rides has been to celebrate fitness and good health and be an example to those who learn from my rides that dreams can be lived. The kids and staff back at Partners in Learning in Salisbury would be waiting to hear that the ride had started. I serve as the Wellness Coordinator there.

I ate a Power Bar, rolled my bike out the door and sat down to ask God to provide the safety that only He could. My pattern developed that day. I got the bike out the door, went back in to make sure nothing was left behind, and sat down to say my prayers. Those prayers always ended with "Lord, ride with me today," just as they had the summer before.

On the bike, I realized that my cyclometer was not working again. I e-mailed our Salisbury bike shop Skinny Wheels, and Eric sent me a reply as to the possible cause. Turns out he was right that the little magnet on the wheel spoke was not lining up exactly with the cyclometer reader because it had been twisted, probably in shipping.

15

Before I had gone 20 miles, I knew my stomach needed more fuel. My very first stop at a convenience netted a huge heated cinnamon bun and some cookies along with a pleasant conversation with the clerk. Now properly fueled, I headed north on Highway 3 and then north and east on US 1, which would soon become an old friend. Many people who had traveled extensively on the East Coast told me that US 1 goes from Maine to Florida and that I could ride it all the way to Key West. Those people were not quite right, but they were correct in that the highway itself does go all that way. I found out later why I couldn't ride the whole way on it, several times in fact.

Immediately, I realized that not only did Maine look like Oregon from the air, it also smelled the same way. I can only describe it as a sweet and musky smell, but very pleasant. The stands of fir trees were not quite as thick in Maine but were still dense enough for me to wonder if a Bigfoot might be watching me. After I left Ellsworth, my route would follow US 1 nearly all the way to Lubec and would become less and less populated along the way.

Just the day before, a cycling resident of this area told me that this part of US 1 scared him, and he wouldn't take a chance on riding it. His reasoning included poor roads, little or no shoulders and plenty of logging trucks. I kept those thoughts in the back of my head as I pedaled ahead. The scenery was pretty from the start, and occasionally I would get a glimpse of the water. Just as in Oregon, when I saw the water closely I was at sea level, meaning that a climb was coming very soon. This pattern lasted throughout the state. Over and over, I climbed to the top of hills and a few small mountains before cresting them and then coasting to the bottom to start the process again. It certainly took much longer to climb the hills that it did to coast down. I preferred to have some flat riding mixed in but almost none of that would occur in the trek to Lubec.

Maine had beautiful old homes, many of them for sale. A common sight was a boat or boats in the front yard and a significant pile of lobster traps beside them. I passed through nice little towns like Jonesboro, Machias and East Machias, the latter two being the specific area that I had been warned about. The day had been a little cool to start and was now very pleasant at midday. I saw only endless hills ahead, repeatedly reaching the top of one only to find another in the near distance ready to be climbed. The roads turned out to be fine, and for most of the day I had plenty of room to ride. Small shoulders kept me out of the traffic lanes, and the volume of traffic was never too heavy. Logging trucks never became an issue. That resident had been worried about the pieces of bark that fly off of them, but none came my way.

I fulfilled a lifelong dream to visit Wild Blueberry Land near Columbia Falls. Well, given how tired and thirsty I was by early afternoon, it seemed like a dream—or a delusional state. Nearly everything is painted blue at Wild Blueberry Land, and most things honor the blueberry. I got some blueberry ice cream and ice cold water, and then perked right up after hearing that I had just over 40 miles left to get to Lubec. It wasn't a day that could be wasted on sightseeing, so I passed another major opportunity when I bypassed the five-mile ride to the Sardine Museum. Some regrets can last a long time, but I bet that one doesn't, even though I meant no intended slight toward those little fish at all. I have told myself over and over that I can't see everything when I pass through on the first trip, so next time I'll visit the Sardine Museum. That museum was just the first of many things that I truly do hope to visit at a later date.

As I went farther north, the homes often were part of farms. Occasionally, the barn would be attached to the house, probably owing to the fact that winters are so cold in the area. I thought of some of my farming friends at home and wondered what they would think of having the dairy cows just a door away. Past residents of Maine had told me about the harsh winters, and I wondered if that might be part of the reason so many homes were for sale or just boarded up.

I kept pedaling and knew from my maps that there was a turn-off onto Highway 189, the road to the Lubec area. By that time, Lubec had almost become mystical, as I wondered what it would be like. Cotton Ketchie had told me not to miss the Lubec area, and I was soon to get there. Closing in on 90 miles, I stopped at a small gift shop and visitor center to make sure I was on the right track. I also wanted to ask whether there was a motel close to the state park that I needed to visit. Pat McCabe told me about one and even called to make sure they would hold a room. She also told me that I was about 10 miles from the motel, which turned out to be almost exact.

I found the motel and realized that I was still at least 4 to 5 miles from the state park and lighthouse. Pat had told me that the volunteer staff at the park didn't stay too late, so she suggested going there early tomorrow. My goal was a picture of the most eastern sunrise in the U.S., so I decided to settle in the motel, eat plenty, get some rest and be ready to go early in the morning. When I inquired at the motel desk about the time of the sunrise and the distance to the park, I was told the sunrise was at 4:50 a.m. and I had a 6-mile ride in the dark to get to the park. After 104 miles for the day, that was the last news I wanted to hear. I had to be up very early. A quick ride to a nearby convenience store netted the food that I needed. Soon, I headed for bed, content with the progress made on the first day but expecting an even bigger challenge the next day.

The ride started at 3:30 a.m., almost entirely closed in by fog. My bike had a flashing red light on the back, and I hoped any cars would see it. Thankfully there was almost no traffic as I made my way to the Quoddy Head State Park and its famous lighthouse. It was dark, cold and foggy, with a chilly wind blowing around me. There had been no wind at all on the road in, but now the fog was blowing by at a rapid rate. I made pictures of the lighthouse with its brilliant light working against that fog and also of the granite slab that had the famous words signifying the most eastern point in the U.S. Not a soul was in sight, and the lighthouse keeper's home was being remodeled and was obviously empty. The fog was thick, and sunrise was approaching, but I knew there was no chance to get a photo at this location. I rode back down the road in a hurry and caught a good photo of the sunrise a couple of miles away.

I rode on through Lubec as the sun continued its ascent. My goal was to explore the town and look across the bay towards New Brunswick and the bridge toward Canada as I searched for the best place to dip the rear tire to officially signify the start of the trip. There had been no one else around the lighthouse to take a photo, plus the dark sea looked so foreboding that trying to get the bike in the water was not possible. As I pedaled around Lubec, I found a group of fishermen loading their boat and asked one of them, Steve Tinker, to take my photo. He jumped at the chance after I told him my purpose, and I soon had the needed photos. Lubec is an old fishing village with 96 miles of coastline and lots more. There are whales, eagles, seals and great hiking trails that celebrate magnificent views. My one regret is that I didn't take my passport, which would have allowed me a short ride over the bridge into Canada. One of the park rangers had even suggested it on the phone a few days before I left North Carolina. I thought it would have been too much trouble to keep up with my passport for a small return. No doubt, I was wrong. The bridge wasn't long, and it would have taken little effort to visit our neighbors to the north for just an hour or so. A quick breakfast in Canada would have been worth telling about. Next time, for sure.

After a brief visit back to the Eastland Motel to load the bike, I hit the road ready for another 100-mile day. Almost immediately I realized there was a slight headwind. Yesterday, the wind had pushed me, and it looked like that same wind would be in my face today. Up and down those same hills I went, heading back south on 189 toward US 1.

My first stop for food was at the intersection of the two high-ways. It was still before 9 a.m., so I got several things to eat in the lodge/convenience store. My debit card was refused when I tried to buy breakfast, marking the fact that someone at my bank had noticed the card was being used far away from home. A call back to my hometown bank took care of that problem. The breakfast included my first brownie on the trip. I was already dreading the hills and retracing my route while the headwind was building. This day would be a challenge. That was OK; challenges would come in all shapes and sizes over the next 35 days. On I pedaled.

I rode doggedly against the unrelenting hills. For the first time in my long-distance riding, I realized I had a huge blister developing on the heel of my right hand. I failed to mention that a staple of my gear is a pair of leather gloves meant to reduce the friction between the handlebars and the hands. The blister was just something that I had to live with for the time being. My first-aid kit on this trip didn't amount to much, and there would be time to address the issue later. My planned stop for the night in Ellsworth seemed so far away, with 60 miles still to go at noon. Only 40 miles completed at this point for someone who had been up since 2:30 a.m. was not good. Having seen the same scenery the day before didn't help any, either.

The miles dragged on, but the wind seemed to relent as the afternoon passed. I was riding southwest on US 1, starting to think of the end of the day. Locals talked about the hot weather, how it had suddenly heated up when the high reached 79. I smiled at the day's high temperature as I pulled into a nice little ice cream stand hoping to get some insight into the motel situation. No one seemed to be able to help until I got to the front of the ice cream line. The two clerks knew all about Ellsworth and had plenty of ideas. Kaylee and Christina called a few places, and we settled on the Knight's Inn. A call ahead told me what to look for and the approximate distance. My ice cream choice that day was blueberry again, and the boost that it provided had to power the last part of the twin-100 mile days. I was admittedly tired and ready to find that motel and get off the bike for the night.

The planned distance of 8 miles turned into 14, but regardless I was soon settled in a very nice motel with a huge thunderstorm threatening. The desk clerk, Nick Umphreys, and I discussed the purpose of my ride and his own battle with obesity as a child. He gave me a quiet room, directed me to the only food in the area at a local dairy bar and asked if he could help me in any way.

The motel was situated at the top of a big hill, and I rode downhill to find the dairy bar, not sure what I could eat. I am usually very strict about my diet and have been a vegetarian for about 30 years. Many of my meals from dairy bars and grills had been limited to grilled cheese sandwiches and potatoes made in the healthiest possible way. That was not a concern, because a car show was going on at the dairy bar, and 40 people must have been in line. Looking at the approaching storm and knowing that my tired legs had no desire to stand in that line, I headed back up to the motel and ate out of my own food reserves and a vending machine. It was a wonderful, restful night as the wind and rain churned outside. I was in the dry after my 103 extremely hard miles for the day. Day two had been much harder than day one for several reasons. The headwind pushed me backward for most of the day, and the sameness of the terrain didn't inspire me as it does when I am riding to new places. Admittedly, I was a little tired from the first day.

When I woke up, a fog had settled over the area following the rains. Fog has never been a friend to cyclists, so I delayed my start a few minutes. I had time to listen to storm damage reported on TV that included some lightning injuries. It was good news that the storms were clearing the area at that time, so I hit the pavement at 7 a.m.

Early towns on the day's ride were East Orland and Bucksport. I crossed a very modern bridge in Bucksport situated beside a still visible Revolutionary War fort. The Americans had taken a resounding defeat at the fort when they attacked it.

I rode on to the town of Stockton hoping to see the lighthouse advertised on Route 1 but was told that the town and lighthouse were separated by 4 miles. By this time, my arms and legs were sore from the two preceding hard days. Next time, I thought. On to Searsport, Belfast and Camden. New England photo opportunities were everywhere, and the ride had become very enjoyable. I began to love pedaling through the old towns. The pace didn't seem very hurried in this area, and I always had plenty of room to ride even though there were very few bike lanes. I felt back in my element. Seeing Maine from the bike seat was just fine with me, and I felt extremely blessed to be able to do it.

Already I was reminded that often car riders don't have the concept of how many miles away something is. The day before, I asked about the distance to Ellsworth from Matthias and was told 45 miles. The correct distance was 65 miles, almost a lifetime in difference to a touring cyclist. Once I started to look for a motel to spend the night, I asked today for the distance to a certain town. "It is about 3 miles, but it might be more since you are on a bike!" Shouldn't it be the same either way? The town was 7 miles, another lesson confirmed! Folks from Maine did all seem very happy to have a cyclist stop in to ask questions, and they often had some of their own. One particular convenience store was so friendly that I went back in to purchase more things that could easily have waited for later.

I spent the night at the Yankee Traveler Motel just south of Warren, Maine. US 1 had lots of older mom-and-pop motels. I began to find some that were very reasonably priced. That would become a trend the farther south I went. Total mileage for this day was 84, with all three of the first days well above my intended daily average. With all the extra miles and the rugged terrain, my legs and arms were already sore. I didn't expect this to last but did know that my body had to get used to pushing hard again. I had said before that there is really no way to train for such riding, and the best way to do it was on the ride itself. This scenario was proving itself once again, just as it had the previous year.

Hurricane Arthur was grabbing headlines in the area. Tomorrow was supposed to have headwinds and several doses of significant rain. I have often ridden in rain and actually enjoy it as long as the wind is not strong in my face at the same time. Fourth of July celebrations, including fireworks and parades, had already been postponed and canceled in the area. I went to sleep wondering what the next day would be like. Only about two more days remained in Maine.

As the sun rose the next morning, I could clearly see it. In fact, few clouds were visible. I hit the road about 6 a.m. hoping to make time while the sun shined. The first town that morning was Waldoboro, with plenty of water and a beautiful bridge. I kept pushing on to Damariscotta, yet another beautiful and historic town with an even longer bridge. Clouds had started to close in, and a slight mist developed. I noticed that with all the continued climbing, my legs were very tired and had not refreshed overnight the way they often do. One guy in a van pulled over in front of me just to tell me that showers were in the area, and I should find a place get out of the anticipated lightning. It was just mid-morning, too early to stop and the wind was not a factor. I had to keep riding but it was certainly nice of him to worry about me.

The next town on US 1 was Bath. Bath is renowned for shipbuilding, having launched over 5,000 vessels. At one time, over 200 shipbuilding firms were located here, as was the nation's fifth-busiest port. As I passed, I realized that the town was going ahead with its Fourth of July parade. I almost stopped, but the threatening weather kept me going. Bath was the only town I passed through that continued on with its Fourth of July Celebration as scheduled. The rains came much later that day, and I felt sure that got the parade completed.

About the same time, US 1 suddenly became four lanes, and it flattened out for the first time on my ride. My pace picked up and my tired legs felt much better, but only until I was pulled over by Officer Goan from the Brunswick Police Department. He told me that cyclists were not allowed on this short portion of the highway, and that I would have to leave US 1 at the next exit and find my way several miles through other roads before I could rejoin US 1. Officer Goan was very professional and a pleasure to talk to, even consenting to have his picture made in front of his cruiser with the blue light flashing. I had never been stopped on a bicycle for any reason, not even on several interstate segments out West. Being pulled over in this case just added to the fun, especially since I was soon released to continue on my journey. Officer Goan sounded the siren and waved as he pulled away.

In the fortunate way that things often happen to me, it was a blessing to get off the highway and ride through Brunswick. I rode past Bowdoin College and probably the most beautiful little town of my whole trip. The long lines of historic homes and perfectly-kept yards were amazing. Quickly, I found my way back to US 1 and headed south again.

Freeport, home of giant retailer L.L. Bean, was next. I rode into town and noticed a McDonald's that was located in a historic home. Next, I found that the sidewalks were crammed with an up-scale crowd, reminding me very much of the Breckinridge, Colo., crowd. Satisfied with my pace for the day, I got off the bike long enough to go inside the L.L. Bean store. Just a few quick peeks at some prices let me know that I didn't need to waste my time. Out the door I went. Rain was now threatening, and I pushed on. This was the only time that I saw crowds of people in Maine. Freeport had jammed sidewalks and plenty of people even with bad weather about to arrive.

Rain soon started to fall in earnest, so I stopped at a visitor center in Falmouth to ask about possible lodging. Two volunteers told me there were about six places coming up and suggested I ask at them. They warned me of high prices because of the trendy group that frequented the area. I found one motel, paid a little too much for not the nicest room, but got out of the now very heavy rain. Total mileage for this day, a Friday, was 77 miles. Tomorrow I would have to leave US 1 and Maine. I slept very well as the windy rain pounded down.

My last day in Maine had arrived. The rain was still falling as I left the motel about 6:30 a.m. Without the rain, I would have spent the night camping. Some forecasts had called for 4-6 inches overnight, but we didn't get that much. The wind was still blowing as I left and headed for Kennebunk, one of the oldest towns in the country. Soon the rain stopped, and Hurricane Arthur had passed us by. Next came Wells and then Moody Beach. Moody Beach was the only example that I saw of a long and pretty beach, having passed many short and rocky beaches so far. The popularity of that beach on a warm day, coupled with few access roads, caused a huge traffic backup. I rode out to the beach, often passing the same cars and joking with the occupants as we saw each other again. One group even had me take a picture of them.

I left Maine as I rode through Kittery. Some of the town is in Maine, and some is in New Hampshire. Goodbye to a wonderful and scenic state and some very nice people. I will visit again.

Chapter 4
— New Hampshire and Massachusetts —

Meeting lots of wonderful people

Just having entered Kittery, still on the Maine side, I asked directions from the proprietor of a furniture store. Not a car was in sight, and when I walked in the store, nobody came out for several minutes. I started to leave, and then a grouchy guy appeared and asked: "What do you want?" I asked how to find the waterfront, and he grunted, "Waterfront. What waterfront? Just keep going over the bridge and you will see plenty of water." Good thing he was still in Maine, because I didn't meet anybody like him in New Hampshire. Thinking back, I didn't meet anybody else like him in Maine either. This brief visit reminded me that not everyone was going to be nice and accommodating. However, by far the largest percentage were, and that has been a constant of all my bike riding.

I left his store quickly and found the bridge, one of several in town. I knew the states divided somewhere over the bridges and looked for the "Entering New Hampshire" sign. After a stop on the other side of the bridge, I asked if this was New Hampshire yet and was assured that I was definitely in New Hampshire now. "Where is the sign?" I asked. The clerk said he didn't know, but he did think that I could ask someone at the bridge. After backtracking, I found the drawbridge operator who told me there was no sign. He was in a hurry because I needed to get off the bridge so he could raise it and allow a boat to pass. So, still looking for a state sign, I rode back into Maine on the other side of the bridge.

Unsure of what to do next, I asked Melissa Baker who waited in her truck at the base of the bridge if she knew about a sign. Melissa said, "Sure, there is one on the next bridge. Over there it is. There is not one on this bridge. I don't know why." She told me how to get to the other bridge, and I headed off toward it. Although I had to backtrack and wind through other streets, it was worth the time to get that photo, and I had it a couple miles later. I was now officially in New Hampshire.

Getting photos of state signs has become important to me. Someday, I want to have proof that I have visited at least all 48 of the continental United States. Finding the state signs out West was easy. They were all posted prominently, and there were not that many different roads. I knew where the state borders were, and celebrated each time that I entered a new one. On the East Coast, finding the state signs was a little harder. On a few roads, the signs simply aren't there. At least twice I had to get the picture of a sign as I was leaving the state instead of when entering. It was better than nothing but not the way I preferred.

A swirling wind had developed and caused me to pedal harder when it blew as a headwind. The hills had lessened a little, and I was thankful for that. The next town up was Exeter, which I reached on Highway 108 after leaving US 1, then found plenty of traffic as I entered town. There was a van just ahead of me, and because of the heavier traffic, I stayed close behind it. I kept thinking that young girls were screaming somewhere, then I noticed at least two girls waving and hollering out of the back window of the van. They were screaming, "Mr. Freeze, Mr. Freeze!" They kept it up until I could pull up beside them at a light. The female driver had the window down, and said, "They say they know you!" Just then the light changed, and they pulled away. I stopped, hoping that they would too. They didn't, and to this day, I have no idea who the girls were.

Hoping the van might pull back around, I took out my map and made sure I knew where the next turn was and waited a few minutes beside the street. Once I was sure the van was not coming back, I decided to head on toward Wyndham, where I hoped to spend the night. I got back on the bike and realized that the back tire was totally flat, and that the brakes were locked on the rim somehow. I couldn't roll the bike forward or backward, so I carried it off the street. The problem was more than I knew how to fix. I remembered a bike shop listed on one of my maps, found the number for Exeter Cycles and called it. Within 5 minutes, a small dump truck pulled up, and I met Devan Harris. Devan is a sales rep who works the northeast bike shops, and recognized me when he got out of the truck. His friend actually had one of my books, "Lord, Ride with Me Today." We talked a little about last year's ride as we unloaded the gear off my bike and put everything on the truck.

Within minutes, I was at the shop and being introduced to everyone. The shop was busy, but Billy Hagerty put my bike on his work stand and went to work on it. Billy got the bike ready to go, gave it a once-over, and we both rode it around the parking lot to try it out. I said goodbye to everyone, got a little advice from Devan about New York City, thanked Billy and owner John Gromek, and then headed back toward my route out of town. It was now past 5 p.m., and I had at least 28 miles to go to reach the motel in Wyndham. Without taking time to correctly figure out the route, I turned the wrong way and rode back past the band shell. Once I realized my mistake, I was several miles down the wrong road. A lady working in her yard told me of a shortcut to make up part of the wasted time, and I took it.

Soon, I was back on Route 111. It was hilly and curvy, and my pace was slow enough that I worried about making Wyndham. There were no other options, so I pushed as hard as I could while the sun dropped lower in the sky. I took the time to say a prayer asking for the strength to push ahead and get off the road before it was dark. Within a couple of miles the road widened, the pavement improved, and I had a bike shoulder. My pace picked up quickly, and I realized there was now hope of a safe arrival. At about 15 miles out, I was dry and thirsty and stopped to get water from a couple who were out in their yard. Andrew and Browyn filled my bottle with ice water and off I went.

With dark setting in, I called the motel and was told there were still five more miles to go. The owner told me to stay on the same road and look for the motel just past a convenience store. With my red flashing light blinking away, I began pedaling for all I was worth. Amazingly, two fireworks celebrations began to brighten the sky in the distance. Somehow, I found more energy to push faster because of the noise and light show. With about three miles to go, the first totally separate bike lane I had seen on the trip began to run beside the road. I jumped onto it and was now a few feet away from traffic. In total darkness, except for the car headlights, I saw the motel on the left and pulled in and was able to finally relax a little. At 101 miles for the day, I was nearly spent. It had been a great day to meet good people, and the scenery had been amazing as well.

My prayer was answered yet again. Even though I didn't get off the bike until past dark, the separate bike lane kept me out of traffic. If the road had stayed the same as it was when leaving Exeter, I probably would have still been riding for an extra two hours or more. Much of that would have been in dark conditions with a lot of traffic. Curves and hills in the dark with no bike lane certainly would have made for hazardous conditions.

Turned out that the convenience store was not actually close to the motel, and I decided not to go back on the road again. A few cookies, Powerbars and some overheated bananas served as my supper that night. The motel manager had in fact saved my room, a special favor because it looked like he had a full house otherwise. Lots of prayerful thanks went up that night. I went to bed near midnight, hoping for an easier day tomorrow.

I woke up without a real plan for what roads to follow this day. The hills had returned as I headed southwest away from the motel, originally following the Adventure Cycling maps. I decided to ask along the way for some options and planned to have an open mind about the best way to proceed. My first town was Nashua, N.H., and I soon realized that my favorite route from the day before had now changed directions. Highway 111 West had become 111 South. That was fine with me, because south had always been one of my favorite words.

Hunger set in pretty soon, and I stopped at a convenience store. Lynn, who was running the store, and Isaac told me about the Nashua Rail Trail that was just ahead. Rail trails are usually pretty flat, fairly straight and scenic, so I was interested. Somehow I missed their directions and rode past the road that would have taken me to the trail, then turned around and headed back with the help of another cyclist. That time I found the trail and started down it. Isaac had thought there was an "Entering Massachusetts" sign on the trail, but I heard from others using the trail that there was not. So with a little more backtracking, I went back out on the highway, found the sign and snapped a photo, and returned to the start of the trail for the second time. One guy, after I told him what I had done, said, "What does it matter?" My reply was simply, "It just does."

The trail was paved but had broken places and other bumpy areas where roots had pushed up the pavement. When my loaded Surly bounced over these places, neither the bike nor I cared for it much. I made my way back down the trail to about where I thought I was in Massachusetts and pushed on.

A few miles later, I met Michael Veit. Michael had a table set up along the rail trail asking people to do their part to keep a pipeline from coming through the area. Realizing that I was not going to have a great day mileage wise, I took the time to sit and talk with Michael about lots of things. We shared many common interests, and he knew a lot about the Carolinas. I got some great information about the upcoming roads and towns, and then once again I headed south.

The rail trail ended in Ayer, so I had to make a decision on how to proceed. The trail had definitely saved a few miles and certainly several large hills. The roads were a little confusing as I headed toward Harvard. I could see that Concord of Revolutionary War fame was easily reachable that afternoon, but the road going there would not allow cyclists. It had become a warm afternoon by that time, and I found Mary Arata working in her yard and playing with her kids. They all had on swimsuits and were spraying each other with a hose. Immediately upon talking with Mary, I knew that she had real insight into the local roads. She suggested that I stay on Highway 111, then head south on Highway 27. She said that excessive traffic and ongoing road construction would make the ride to Concord more dangerous than it should be. Mary said that I would enjoy 27, which had plenty of room to ride a bike. I took a few photos and thanked them all, and headed south to follow her suggestions.

It turned out that Mary had provided exactly the right information. Though the Massachusetts roads were not the best, the scenery along Highway 27 was absolutely beautiful as I rode past historic homes, farms and churches on the way to Natick. Natick is on the famed Boston Marathon course, and so is next door Framingham. I rode through Natick and asked a few helpful folks where I might find a reasonable motel. The best advice came from a convenience store operator who said, "I used to live for weeks at a time in all of them. If you will ride about 4 more miles to Framingham, there are several good options." Another perfect call, and I spent the night in a huge motel in Framingham, just across the street from a Walmart, McDonald's and a grocery store. My mileage on this day totaled only 68, but with the backtracking and all the conversations that actually saved time, I was happy with my progress. Once again, I went to bed with no firm plan as to how to continue south.

Since I had run the Boston Marathon course four times, it was especially nice to revisit the area. My last Boston race was in the '90s, so quite a bit had changed. The towns of Natick and Framingham were still small and full of history. I enjoyed seeing a little bit more of them this time. While running competitively, you seldom look around much, and that was certainly the case as I ran through both towns years before. Now that I am older and don't race much, my runs are slower and full of curiosity. I look around at everything and enjoy all there is to hear and smell. It is the most fun when I can do the same things on a bike as well, but being on wheels sometimes requires much more concentration on those around me. Natick and Framingham were just busy enough that I had to keep my thoughts on traffic and watch the road, but still I knew that both towns would have been fun to visit for much longer.

The next morning, I headed back into Natick and decided to stop for a good map that included Massachusetts, Rhode Island and Connecticut. I could tell that I needed to head south as well as west through these states to eventually continue south through New York City and New Jersey. Adventure Cycling offers only an option to take a side trip to New Jersey and access New York City through the ferries or other public transportation. I already thought I wanted to do more.

Most days were now becoming a series of decisions on how to proceed. I wanted to stay away from the worst traffic but still head in the proper direction to eventually visit my target cities. Actual maps and mapquest.com provide very little information on the best roads for cyclists. I began to search out small roads that were headed in the right direction and that didn't intersect with major highways. My journey was now squarely inside a heavily populated corridor, and virtually any road would be busy. No more roads where cars were few and far between. Often, I just made my best guess and pedaled on. Most of those decisions turned out just fine.

Out of Natick, I continued in a southwest direction on Highway 27, then a little more west on Highway 16. My cyclometer quit working again, or at least stopped doing what I needed most. It was registering the speed but not the total mileage. As mentioned before, the mileage between towns and turns is important so that the cyclist knows where he or she needs to start looking for specific road names. Total mileage was often the number one parameter that graded my day's work. I had to keep up with it. For just the few hours that my cyclometer didn't work, I felt a little naked without all the information that was needed to make those better decisions.

Milford was the next town, and a stop at a dog trainer's shop told me there were two bicycle shops nearby. One was in his same building but was closed on Mondays. This just happened to be a Monday. I proceeded on to the next one, Milford Bicycle, and stopped to see whether my cyclometer could be repaired or whether the problem resulted from something I was not doing correctly. About half an hour later, I left with a new cyclometer of a different type. Because of the difference in registering mileage, I thought it was not working and returned to the shop for more instruction. I was told to change to a different mode to get the total miles, and once again I headed south. Milford is known as the Granite Town in the Granite State because of the various quarries and was also a stop on the Underground Railroad.

On to Uxbridge, with one of the largest collections of historic homes and churches in the area, and I took time to look around. I stopped often to make photos and eventually stopped again for lunch and to formulate my plan for the rest of the day. I decided to ride through the northwest portion of Rhode Island on the way into Connecticut. Carrie Smith and Norman Labelle in Douglas gave me some insight into how to do it. I enjoyed meeting them after I spotted Norman's tow truck parked in front of Carrie's shop. Anytime that I needed directions and spotted a tow truck around, I have had great success in getting the proper information.

So far the day had been dragging a little, and I decided to stop at an ice cream shop to recharge. On a long day of meeting special people, I spotted two loaded bikes already parked beside the shop. Bret Ericson and Katie Levin would be only the second and third long-distance cyclists that I had seen on the trip to this point. They told me they were cycling north from Brooklyn, N.Y., to Portland, Maine. We shared insight on the roads that we both had used as well as available motels and bike shops. Bret and Katie told me about a long rail trail that led from Brewster, N.Y., directly into the Bronx, in New York City. I questioned them at length about this and how I could then exit the city and continue south. With this conversation, a seed of thought was planted. I really wanted to ride into New York City on a bike.

Part of the reason that I loved these two rides so much is the chance to do something unusual and slightly daring. New York City on a bike, even if for no more than half a day, would be fun. I know the locals have made good use of bicycles, and for just a short time, I wanted to be a part of that.

Bret and Katie headed north, and I continued south. We communicated by e-mail while monitoring each other's progress over the next few days and eventually kept in touch through the ends of our respective journeys.

Rhode Island was on the horizon, and still one more special person helped me get there. I met Bill Raymond of Harrisville, R.I., out on the road. He was out cycling and stopped while waiting for traffic at a corner. It was a perfect time for me to ask him about the area. Bill had lived in Rhode Island for many years but had recently returned after living and working in Greensboro, N.C. I crossed into Rhode Island just a few miles later following Bill's suggested route.

Chapter 5
— Rhode Island and Connecticut —

More freelance riding

Most of us know that Rhode Island is the smallest state in the United States but not much more about it than that. I had never been to Rhode Island, thus joining Maine, New Hampshire and Connecticut as other states that were new to me on this journey.

Rhode Island has been known for its support for freedom of conscience and action, often defying authority along the way. Religious freedom was important to early settlers, including Roger Williams. It was the first British colony to declare its independence but the last of the original 13 states to ratify the Constitution. Rhode Island chose not to participate actively in the War of 1812.

After the discussion with Bill Raymond of Harrisville, I headed that way. As soon as I left Massachusetts and headed into Rhode Island, the roads immediately improved. I had a nice time in Massachusetts but won't miss the roads at all, especially the ones in the bigger towns.

On the way to Harrisville, I developed a broad plan for the rest of the day. I wanted to follow a good road called Route 44 into Connecticut. While Bill made it sound easy to connect with Route 44, it didn't turn out that way. On the way into Harrisville, I came upon a man who had a disabled motorcycle parked beside the road. He already had a truck and trailer there and appeared to be working on the motorcycle. I asked if I could help, and he told me, "No, I am just trying to decide what to do next." I thought he might be under the influence of something, as his answers were slurred and not always to the point. Still, I asked him about my intended plan and quickly realized that I was just wasting time listening to the long and rambling answer. When he finally took a breath, I said thanks and goodbye, then headed for the nearby firehouse.

There were several volunteer firemen washing trucks, and they all seemed interested in my ride. I was surprised that they didn't know much about Route 44 and Putnam, Conn. One of them went to get his supervisor, and from him I got a confirmation on how to get through town and out to 44. Road signs seemed to disappear through town, and I made at least one wrong turn and had to backtrack. It was also a hilly route, and I once more became unsure about the right street. I stopped and asked, this time approaching a homeowner working in his yard. His positive response was, "Yes, this is the right road. You bicycle riders come by here all the time." We talked for a while and he told me that he thought Putnam was about 30 miles away. By this time, it was mid-afternoon and getting warm. Needing something cold to drink, I stopped at the only convenience store in sight, just as I got to Route 44. While making my purchase, I asked the young clerk, "How far to Putnam?" He said he wasn't sure but thought the distance to be 6 miles. My maps showed it to be more, and a customer in the store agreed. I asked the customer about available motels, and he told me about one that I would pass on the way to Putnam.

I am always wary of entering a convenience store that has bars on the windows and doors. Given a choice, I always go to the one without any bars and the one with the most traffic. This particular convenience store had the bars and was heavily stocked with things that I would never buy. I found a couple of snack items and then approached the young clerk to ask him more about the distance to Putnam. He wanted to be helpful and immediately took out his phone and started expanding the screen as he pulled up a map. Putnam is the next town over, and I couldn't believe that he would not at least have a ball park idea of how far I had to go. Then he said, "About six miles." I was immediately thankful for his effort but knew that the information was just about useless. I hoped for his sake that he keeps his eyes and ears open to learn about things around him and does not rely on his phone for all the answers.

Route 44 turned out to be a good road, with plenty of room for me to ride. I passed a few campgrounds but never saw the motel previously mentioned. I kept riding over moderate hills and eventually passed into Connecticut. I reached Putnam, just over 14 miles from the convenience store. The distance was way more than the 6 miles predicted by the store clerk but considerably less than the 30 suggested by the homeowner. So far, this had been an afternoon of confusion, and I still didn't have a place to spend the night.

My first stop was a mega gas station, but one of those with only a little booth in the middle that housed the operator. A quick conversation with him about motels resulted in his answer, "I have no idea. I am not from around here." I asked a driver getting gas who didn't know either. Just then, the Yatev family pulled in. They all jumped out, and we took photos and talked. John and Alaina, mom and dad, knew just where I should go and gave easy directions. They pointed me on toward Dayville, out near the interstate highway. Their kids, Johnny and Lila, seemed to be genuinely excited about meeting me. I wanted to hit the road, and John said, "If you get lost, just ask for directions to the Burger King or give us a call. Everybody around here knows where it is. Remember, the motel is at the top of the hill." That ended up being a very prophetic statement.

John and Alaina actually inspired me as I listened to them talk to their kids about what I was doing. The whole family was excited about helping me and talking about the ride. As often happens, they asked if they could take me to the motel. Of course, I had to decline but felt deep down that they understood why I couldn't accept. Perhaps because of their kids' memories of me, a few more dreams will come true in the future.

With the sun dropping toward the western horizon, I finally found the Burger King after a sometimes challenging road. Actually, the inclines came early and then a lot of downhill while coasting toward the crossroad below the motel. I looked to the left and saw the road climbing dramatically. The motel itself was not in sight, but a sign about it was. I decided to stop and get some food before making the climb. No need to do it twice.

After packing some food in my bags, I headed up the hill, by far the most challenging of the day. The hill was steep, and my eventual reward was spotting the Budget Inn, still ahead but sitting on a plateau. I chose the first driveway to enter simply because I didn't want to continue uphill to the second. The Yatev family was right. I got a good deal and a comfortable room. Turns out the owner's dad had bought the motel on top of the mountain many years before, and it had remained in the family ever since. That owner loved the idea of my ride and spent quite a while talking about the logistics of it.

Total mileage for today was about 70, with part of it estimated because of the broken cyclometer. I never looked at the Adventure Cycling maps all day, largely because I liked the route that all my new friends had helped me put together.

Up early the next morning after a restful night, I headed out and realized how great the view was from the Budget Inn parking lot. I had to get my feet in the pedal cages quickly because the downhill was even more dramatic than the previous day's uphill ride. At the bottom of the hill, I stopped for a few food items and a more detailed Connecticut map at the best convenience store. Since Connecticut is situated north and east of New York City, I had to continue moving slightly south and more west than on some of the previous days. Many of Connecticut's better roads don't allow bicycles, so I asked the store clerk his ideas on how to proceed. We settled on Route 12 south and then Route 6 west to begin the day. I did not expect the challenging ride that I would get as I rode away from the store.

Route 12 was fine, but the turn onto Route 6 brought hill after challenging hill. My pace slowed, sometimes averaging less than 7 miles per hour. I had plenty of time to analyze whether I still needed some of the things in my bags and eventually decided to sort out some items that I could ship home to lighten the load. The morning dragged by slowly as I reached the middle part of Connecticut near Willimantic on Highway 66. Roads in Connecticut were generally pretty good, but the larger towns had lots of potholes and much road repair needed. It was the first time in several days that I was in a bigger city, and it took a little getting used to.

Bigger cities were less personal and scenic than the small towns that I had already visited. Streets often needed repair, and the populations were much more diverse. More trash and debris were in or near the roadway, so I had to keep my eyes on what might be passing under my tires as well. Most importantly, I had to be focused and ready for what the traffic might do around me.

The same theme continued as I entered Middletown. Suddenly the roads became very busy, and the shoulder that I needed quickly disappeared. The temperature had reached 90 degrees, adding to the stress of the moment. I pushed on, listening for the first time to multiple big city horns that never seemed to cease. I crossed a major bridge while riding in heavy traffic, causing a tow truck driver to slow and blow his horn before yelling, "Ride on the sidewalk!" Some cities do encourage cyclists to ride on the sidewalk, but others are happy to cite you for doing the same thing. I continued to ride in the street, though later I saw a few casual cyclists on the sidewalks.

After making a major right turn, I spotted a grassy hill and pulled over to park my bike for a few minutes and get a drink while studying my maps. I sat in the shade of a large tree, which lowered the air temperature significantly. For just a minute, I laid my head back and was nearly asleep when Patrick Glass rode up to ask where I was headed. Patrick was a student at Wesleyan University in Middletown and had come from California by way of Maine to continue his education. He was a great guy, and I enjoyed our discussion that afternoon.

Meeting these people often made me wonder about how they ended up in the town where I met them and what their lives had been like. Patrick had already been across the country for his education and even at his young age was very interesting. I am always curious about people and had mentioned before that it would be great fun to return at a later date and try to find those who are mentioned in my books. What fun it would be to walk up to as many as I could find and simply hand them a book!

Soon, I had to leave the shade and start climbing more hills. I chose to stop in Meriden, Conn., just a little after 5 p.m. My distance was only 60 miles for the day, but all of those were well earned with the potholes, building traffic and never ending hills.

I bought a detailed New York State map, complete with several insets of New York City. There was a diner next to the motel with a sign that always gets my attention—Breakfast All Day! The diner evidently had a long history of serving famous people, and it was fun to look around at the pictures. I ordered Belgian waffles and an egg sandwich. The waffles were huge, way bigger than any that I had seen before. I can't remember the last time I was so full, even after a long day on the bike. Another positive about Meriden was that the Yankees were covered on local TV. It was fun to visit there.

The next morning, I headed out following a road plan devised using MapQuest. The route called for about 20 turns, and when the third turn was not there, I had to improvise. While traveling on a bike, I often have found myself wondering if I am on the right road. The best routes have few turns and long sections on the same road. Less worry about the route and more time to enjoy the scenery and the ride are the result. On this particular morning, I was stopped and looking confused at an intersection when Karen walked by. She must have noticed that I needed help, so she took time to reassure me that my route plan was still good. Her next words were frightening, "You know you have a couple of mountains to climb?" Of course I didn't, but now these words were all I could think of.

Those mountains were the roads leading out of town, some of the toughest climbing on the trip to that point. They wouldn't be the last for the day.

I headed over to Waterbury, another bigger town. Somehow I ended up on the wrong side of town and had a long haul to cross through it. Unsure of how to proceed, I spotted a tow truck driver who said, "Yes, I know all those roads, and you are headed the right way. Stick with it." I used Meriden Road and Highway 322.

When finally through town, I had a short and very enjoyable flat stretch. A bike shop was on my right, and I decided to stop and talk about my long-range plans to get into New York City. The shop wasn't open yet, but the owner came out from a building across the parking lot. I met Bobby Sprocket that day, who just happens to have the perfect name for a bicycle shop owner. Bobby was a very fit looking cyclist, so I was confident he would have some great information. Bobby was also personable and had a grin when he told me about a huge hill coming up that local riders used for hill training. "Not another one!" I thought, but of course I kept that to myself.

The big hill Bobby mentioned was the very worst of the whole Maine to Florida ride without a doubt. Few in the Rockies were as steep. I finally had to get off and push the bike to the top, something I hate to do. A runner was actually running the hill, but truth is he was walking as fast as could. We talked for a little bit at the top of the hill, where I was told that only a series of hills in Vermont were steeper. I pushed on through several turns and crossed Interstate 84 several times. My goal was Danbury, and I just kept pedaling in that direction. A visit to Lake Zoar and a huge old steel bridge provided a short, less hilly respite from all the climbing.

Just a few minutes later, I was amazed to ride into Sandy Hook, Connecticut. Sandy Hook was the site of the school tragedy that garnered worldwide attention. Sandy Hook is a very small, historic town centered on a scenic small river. The town is so compact that I rode in from the north on a downhill, crossed the small river and headed out of town to the south on a huge uphill. I kept wondering about the long-term effects on the residents of the town and offered another prayer as I rode into Newtown, Sandy Hook's larger neighbor, on yet one more exhausting hill.

I wanted to find Route 6 and figured I had a little ways to go yet. About that time, I spotted a police officer on his bicycle and rode over to him. I asked Officer Penna the best way to Danbury and whether there was anything in particular that I needed to know. We enjoyed a nice conversation as we rode together to the top of another huge hill, but Officer Penna knew how to cut through a church parking lot to lessen the long climb. Officer Penna told me that he is on bike patrol only during the summer and enjoyed it a lot. His bike was more of a mountain style, and I sure can tell why. Good thing he doesn't have to strap on a bunch of extra weight when riding around town.

Route 6 took me into Danbury where the road signs became a little confusing, so a quick conversation with two interested firefighters told me what to look for. They offered to let me stay in the firehouse overnight, but I declined only because I wanted to make more miles. Tanisha Watson suggested that I check the Super 8 ahead in Mill Plain. I did just that, and after checking in, I made a quick run down to the local grocery store and got back just ahead of a huge downpour. The owner happened to be at the desk when I came back and told me that I couldn't take the bike into my room, to which I replied, "Well then, I will have to stay somewhere else. Give me my money back." The owner changed his tune quickly when his desk clerk told him about my ride, and soon told me what he knew about North Carolina. This was another restful night with the rain coming down. Total mileage was again 60 miles today as I battled the hills. I rested that night, just two miles from the New York State border. Connecticut hills were in the past, leaving behind the hilliest state that I encountered.

Of course, I could not leave the bike outside. In all of my travels,

I had been told only about three times that I couldn't keep the bike in my room. The bike is my transportation, and all the accessories are what made the ride possible. I felt that I had no choice but to leave when told that I couldn't keep my bike with me nor have it locked up in a safe place that was accessible by early morning.

My riding was going to take a change of significant note for the next few days. So far, I had been comfortable with the traffic around me, and help was reasonably close by if I needed it. Sometime the next day, I would enter New York City. At that point, I would be surrounded by an excess of everything, most notably traffic and people. There had been a gradual buildup of both but nothing extreme yet. Tomorrow I would see those extremes. What would it all be like? Just a day later, and I would find out.

Chapter 6
— New York and New Jersey —

Looking for a New York state of mind

On Thursday, July 10, and the overall 10th day of my trip, I was really excited about what adventures might happen in the next couple of days. I had loved New York City during numerous visits, a few for business, but the most notable being for New York Yankee baseball and four New York City Marathons. In fact, my very first marathon was in the Big Apple, so I had a special place in my heart for the city that never sleeps. Still, I remained apprehensive about my first arrival on a bicycle, realistic enough to know that there would probably be a few ups and downs throughout the day.

Adventure Cycling does not take its riders into the city, though it does provide an option to visit by public transit. I wanted to ride a bicycle in the city at least once in my life. Today would be that day.

For the last four days, I had been positioning myself to arrive in Brewster, N.Y., early on this morning. I left Mill Plain looking for the "Welcome to New York" sign. The desk clerk the night before had said the border was only two miles away. I found that sign, made my picture about 7 a.m. and headed for Brewster. Brewster had the trail head for the rail trail described so accurately by Bret Ericson when I met him and Katie at the ice cream shop several days previously.

It was nine miles to Brewster, and another one or so to the other side of town where the trail started. The town was waking up, traffic was moderate, and I had to climb a few hills to reach the higher elevation of the trail head. I joined the trail and started south on the first of 53 planned miles to reach the Bronx. Daniel Fritsche joined me on his bicycle, and we talked about my trip and eventually about what I should expect on the trail and in the city. Daniel was from nearby Carmel and had vast knowledge that he was willing to share before he left the trail.

The paved rail trail was in decent shape and had only minor hills. My first hour of riding went very well, but things quickly changed just before the 20-mile mark. I saw people riding back toward me, warning that the trail was blocked and there was no way to get through. Ever the optimist, I continued on, willing to carry the bike if necessary. The overnight storms in the area had been windy enough to damage a significant group of large hardwoods, completely blocking the trail and the woods on both sides. There was no way to get through, and I had to retrace my last couple of miles, far enough to access a paved road that went out to the highway. I stopped twice to find a way around the damage and finally two knowledgeable residents who provided me with the answer. All I could think about was the time that I was losing and couldn't spend in the city because of these delays. Eventually, I hit the trail again and rolled on.

The trail itself is called the Old Putnam Rail Trail and was once the New York Central Railroad Putnam Line, which carried passengers and freight from the Bronx to Putnam County. Service existed between 1881 and 1958.

About four miles from the Bronx, the trail suddenly became dirt with some rail timbers still in the ground. Riding became much harder, especially with the mud from the recent rains. I passed the oldest golf course in the nation just as a cyclist pulled up beside me on a path barely wide enough for one bike, hardly two. George Pickel began a conversation about my overall ride and then about what I planned once I entered the city. Soon he rode on with the profound words, "Be very careful." I finished the last two miles of the trail, and the trees opened up into Van Cortlandt Park in the Bronx. George was sitting there on his bike and said, "If it is OK, I would be glad to lead you over to the Hudson River." I immediately realized that he was saving me a bunch of stress because all I knew to do was to keep working west. George and I talked when we could as we rode ahead, sometimes reduced to single file but always signaling our intentions to turn. He knew exactly which turns to make, and within a few minutes he stopped at a huge set of steps. George told me that I only had to walk the bike to the top of the stairs, and I would find the bikeway along the Hudson River. He also pointed to the George Washington Bridge, my gateway to New Jersey. George told me he was glad that I was riding for childhood obesity because at one time he had been one of those kids. George had worked for the New York City school system as a physical education teacher for several years and has been reminded every day of the childhood obesity problem. We shook hands, wished each other "safe travels" and he rode away. I climbed the stairs, not a particularly easy task with a loaded bike.

I rode downhill on a very crowded bikeway, looking at the river and New Jersey on the opposite shore. Once the bikeway flattened out along the river, I got closer to the bridge and realized it was way back up above me. I rode under the bridge and briefly rolled on down into upper Manhattan. There was no time for sightseeing, requiring me to turn around and head back toward the bridge. Next time, I will ride all the way down to Battery Park and the Statue of Liberty area. I wouldn't be afraid to spend a lot of time on a bicycle in New York City. Many people do. One of my fantasy jobs if I was much younger would be a bicycle courier in that great city. The most fun might be living there for a baseball season and seeing as many Yankee games as I could afford.

I am simply a born and bred country boy, but New York City has always excited me tremendously. Every visit over the years had something special. One of the most memorable was a visit to the Twin Towers just three weeks before they came down on Sept. 11, 2001. We were in town to see the Yankees play and stayed in the hotel that was part of the towers. Because of that visit, many of the scenes we later saw on TV were so much more personal.

After walking my bike back up to the level of the bridge entrance, I mounted up and had to ride several blocks just to find the bike entrance to the bridge. After lots of turns, I made it and started across. The view of the Manhattan skyline was phenomenal, and I stopped to make several pictures. Other cyclists were riding across the bridge as well, all of us using the protected bike path. There was no threat from automobiles though we could see the tremendous double-decker bridge's heavy volume of traffic very well. Walkers and runners joined with the cyclists, but there was plenty of room for all.

After crossing the bridge, I went to Strictly Cycles bike shop to get some guidance on how to work my way through New Jersey and head toward Pennsylvania. I threw them for a loop because they were clearly not used to long-distance cyclists visiting the shop. Strictly Cycles catered to upper-end road and racing bikes. There was not a reference to a touring bike in the place. Though everyone was very nice, it took quite a while for me to get some information that might help as I turned south once again. During all of this, my mind was racing with all the extra challenges. I forgot to get a picture of the New Jersey sign on the bridge, so I went back up on it and returned to New York just long enough to get that photo. Once I had it, I returned to the New Jersey end of the bridge, ready for possibly the biggest challenge so far in the trip.

Just before I left the bridge, I saw two young guys making photos of each other and the bridge. I stopped and told them what I was doing, and they made a couple of pictures of me with the GW Bridge in the background. They became so excited that they both had to have a picture with me too. That boosted my spirits for the very challenging next few hours.

I determined to follow the instructions that I got from Vito at Strictly Cycles for the rest of the afternoon. I ended up getting directed to the same streets several times, and there were a multitude of turns. Frustrated with the directions and my inability to follow the changing street names, I stopped for verbal directions several times. No one could understand English, particularly in an area of Palisades that seemed to be all Oriental. Streets often changed names but remained the same street. One-way streets also messed up my understanding of what to do. The only certainty was that I was headed south, and there was some solace in that.

The thought struck me that maybe I should find a room and then get a good plan together. I would be in New Jersey for only one more day anyway. In over 5,000 miles of long bike trips, I had never been as confused about how to proceed. Luckily, I found a man putting decals on a van and celebrated that he understood English! He told me about a nearby Day's Inn. I left Grand Avenue and eventually found the Day's Inn, though I had to ride the wrong way on a one-way street to get there. A storm was building to the west and seemed headed for the area, adding urgency to the matter as the sun started to set. I inquired about the cost of the room and was told $159 a night, three times what I had been paying. Nobody spoke understandable English. The desk clerk told me, or at least I think he did, that there was a bar on the next corner, and they had food. Then he also told me that I could not bring my bike into the motel. I left, wondering what my next move could possibly be.

My second angel of the day was waiting in the Day's Inn parking lot. I spotted a man sitting in a van with a pleasant look on his face while going over some papers, though I fully expected he couldn't speak English. Alex Yu became my hero that afternoon. I told him why I was in New Jersey on a bike and what I needed to do. He asked me what the desk clerk had told me at the Day's Inn, and Alex then said, "That is ridiculous. You can get a good room on Grand Avenue, and it will probably cost $40-50 a night." Alex told me how to get back to Grand Avenue and told me to head south. "You will start seeing the motels," he said. I thanked him and rode off, never expecting to see Alex again.

The traffic on Grand Avenue was running about 45-50 miles per hour in a 35-mph zone, and I squeezed by on the white line with no shoulders. Sometimes, I had to just close my eyes and keep riding. As 8 p.m. approached, the storm had abated, but I had not found any motels. I saw a woman standing next to her car in the Waste Management parking lot, and I rode over to ask her for help. But as she saw me coming, she jumped into her car, locked the doors and looked at me in terror as she dialed her phone. I just put my hands up and rode on, wondering what about my appearance might have scared her so much. I clearly was on a bicycle and wearing bicycle clothes and a helmet. I saw the environment she worked in, and there were so many more reasons besides me to be afraid.

At that very moment, Alex Yu reappeared, similar to Superman in my time of need. He pulled in and motioned me to keep riding. I did, and just over the next hill was the first motel! I was tired, mentally used up and ready to end the day. I rode into the motel and found Alex there waiting. He sat in the van while I walked in to get a rate for the night from the very attractive desk clerk. I think it was $65, with a $5 charge to get a remote. When I related this to Alex, he offered an idea. "There are a bunch more," he said. "Can we put your bike in the van and go see what they charge?" I agreed, and we rode down the street, stopping and checking the others. Some were full, some were scary looking, and one was dedicated exclusively to social services recipients.

I thought back to all of the good deals on nice places to stay that I had found so far. I don't like sealed off windows that greet the customers inside many of the motels. All of these seedy motels had them, and from the looks of many who were behind the windows, it might have been for the protection of customers. None had pleasing personalities, either, but because of the way the motels looked outside, I probably had already formed an opinion.

I told Alex, "Let's just go back to the first place. It looked clean, and they had a room." Alex agreed, and we headed back that way.

Little did I know what was going to happen next. When we stopped, I went in to see if they still had the room. A different desk clerk told me they did, which I relayed to Alex. We unloaded the bike, right back where we had started. I felt good about that anyway, because if one of the other places was where I spent the night, then I would have to backtrack to cover the miles on the bike. Darkness was closing in quickly.

I thanked Alex, who told me that he and his wife lived nearby and that he traveled these streets several times a day. I thanked him again and offered money for the time and gas, but Alex would not hear of it. We shook hands and waved good-bye as he drove away, once again in the speeding traffic.

Back in the motel office, I told a different and also very attractive girl at the desk that I wanted a downstairs room. She responded that all of the downstairs rooms were booked. I said, "Could you not move somebody who hasn't checked in yet?" The clerk thought a few seconds, and I thought I detected a little smile when she said, "Yes, I can do that."

After paying the $5 fee to get the remote, I took my room key and the bike and went to the room, which I hadn't previously seen. I turned the light on, so glad to be in a motel room for the night. I realized quickly that my room was of a "special" type. The walls were mostly mirrors and so was the ceiling. More mirrors were in the shower, and there was adjustable lighting. The TV was connected to a DVR player, and there were containers of special oils and fragrances on the sink. The room was very clean and well-kept. I opened the door and looked out. Not another person was in sight, though there were some cars in the lot.

With a smile, I walked to the 7-Eleven next door and got some food to eat while sending my report into the paper. On the way back, and for the first time, I noticed the sign along the street. There were special rates for three- and five-hour stays. I wondered whether all the other downstairs rooms were like mine, and whether there was unusual activity going on in them. It honestly didn't matter to me. I would get a good night's sleep and head south once again in the morning. One thing for sure, the trip had livened up, and my 83 miles for the day were almost forgotten.

Up early again, I wanted to beat the traffic as much as I could. Expecting large volume, I was out with my red light flashing (which seemed appropriate) and prepared to pedal off down the street just about dawn. My prayer that morning included a few extra lines, just as on the previous morning. But before I rode away, I turned in my remote for the $5 refund and waited while yet another young and attractive lady took a room for three hours at 6 a.m. My last sight of her was as she walked toward the room holding hands with a well-dressed young man.

Of course, none of this was reported in the dispatches sent back to my hometown paper. Others might have been bothered to spend the night in such a place, but it did not concern me at all. I was in the room for only about nine hours. The bed slept well, and there was no sign of what it was more often used for. Furthermore, I was out of options for the night at the point that I decided to stay here. It was a night that I will never forget, but I will always wonder what the $5 charge for the remote was all about. Do people, after their special rates for three and five hour stays, leave with the remotes?

The initial riding was simple enough. Following a plan formulated the night before, I stayed on Grand Avenue. I wanted to again hook up with the Adventure Cycling maps at some point later that day by heading toward Conshohocken, in Pennsylvania. For some reason this morning, some singing and a few Baptist hymns came to mind.

My street had become Tonelle Avenue, and as the traffic built in volume, I hugged the white line even more. My prepared route called for me to ride over a huge bridge that was under repair, so I stopped and asked the bridge attendant whether I could do that. Ron Thorword told me that I could probably get across the bridge, but I would have a very hard time on the other side. More prophetic words!

I had to walk down a long set of wooden steps with my loaded bike to get off the bridge while lugging close to 80 pounds that morning. I held the brakes as I eased it down the steps, ending in a construction yard for the bridge. My best water bottle fell, and I thought it was gone forever. Finally, I reached the bottom of the steps and found my way out of the construction gate. I was even able to retrieve the water bottle before leaving. Back on the bike, I couldn't find the street that I wanted and asked at a local truck stop if anybody could tell me how to get there. Two very nice drivers talked to me about it and asked where I eventually wanted to arrive. My destination by the end of the day was Pennsylvania, and I told them I thought the best route was US 22 toward Hillside, N.J. They agreed and offered a plan: "Go up on this next bridge and walk across it on the pedestrian walkway." Then get on US 1 and 9 and pedal like heck until you see the US 22 exit. It is only about five or six miles, but US 1/9 is a major expressway. Don't get caught on that road! And be careful."

It was time to take another chance. I followed their directions and somehow got on the expressway. I started pedaling for all I was worth, and a cut from a recent surgery opened up and started bleeding. I had to keep pushing and find US 22; the bleeding could be fixed later. I rode with thousands of cars in rush hour, passing right by Newark International Airport. The saving grace was plenty of room in the breakdown lane. My hope was that I would not be the one who broke down and that no policeman or state trooper would notice me. The US 22 exit sign was another welcome sight, and soon I headed down that ramp.

On the way toward Hillside, I hugged the white line once again as everyone was speeding by. Riding here may have been even scarier than the time spent on Grand Avenue in New Jersey. Fast drivers flew past me for much of the morning. Most of the motorists' possible turns to the left were blocked by concrete barriers for close to 40 miles so that the tremendous volume of traffic would move along better. There were occasional stoplights which did serve to slow them down some. I contemplated stopping at a McDonald's for breakfast once but couldn't get across the road due to the volume of traffic. Ignacio Lopez called out to me while I waited and asked where I was headed. He was an endurance cyclist and bike mechanic and had also biked part of my current trip, plus he lived in the area. Iggy told me what to expect as I got closer to Pennsylvania. He gave me his number, telling me to call if I had trouble, and I pedaled on. Thinking that I might stop, he was waiting for me as I coasted into the next McDonald's on my side of the road. We had a nice breakfast and good conversation before I headed on south.

My last major turn was onto US 202, where the traffic finally started to thin and return to a more reasonable pace. I had no problems, and beautiful weather made for a nice day as the hills gradually started to increase.

The traffic lessened rather dramatically as I approached the Delaware River and the joint toll booth of New Jersey and Pennsylvania. That area was beautiful as I got nearer the river, and I stopped to take a few pictures of the river. A worker at the toll booth came out and started hollering at me to come on to the toll booth. He said, "Don't stop now. You aren't supposed to be on that bridge!"

I rolled on up to Mr. Toll Booth Man and asked what the problem was. He said, "No bicycles are allowed on this road or that bridge." I thought he was joking, and I laughed at him as I described my day so far. Mr. TBM then told me that since I was no longer in New Jersey he couldn't do anything about me now. I asked where the "Welcome to Pennsylvania" sign was. "There just isn't," he replied. I thought, "Yes, just the same as your fantasy 'No Bicycles' sign." I laughed again as I rode away and said goodbye to New Jersey.

I survived the time in the crazy New Jersey atmosphere of rushed traffic and very little room to ride. It would be many more miles before I would face the same kind of traffic again, and I was ready for a break from it. My bike was working well, and I continued to feel strong and confident. The journey was certainly becoming very memorable for its challenges. There was nowhere else that I would rather be.

Chapter 7
— Pennsylvania —

The Amish country and the last of the big hills

After leaving Mr. Toll Booth Man, I headed into Pennsylvania, once again with no real idea of where I might stay. I stopped at a Giant food store, my first one of those. I asked several people, including one of the store managers, about the possibility of a motel. Everybody that I spoke to had the same opinion. There were no reasonably priced rooms in the area. A few people suggested some of the higher priced chains as the only option. Robert from the store stepped up and made a couple of calls. He sent me toward Doylestown, still on US 202, and then north for a four-mile off-route ride to get to the motel. By this time, I've learned that if the motel is away from town, I need to stop and get my food first. It's way too hard mentally to double back for miles just to get food. This was the first motel that, when I asked for ice, I was handed a bowl and two ice trays. Still, the room was plenty good, very comfortable and best yet, it was about half the price of the others around.

I thought I wanted to ride a little off route to pass through Delaware, basically just to add another state to the trip. I went to bed thinking that this plan was best, but then woke up and totally changed it. Early Saturday morning, I came up with a better and more direct route. I would save Delaware for another time.

Since today was July 12 and my youngest daughter's birthday, I called her early that morning when I stopped at another Giant grocery to fill my bags. Virtually no food was left in them since I'd wolfed down my remaining provisions the previous night. Retracing my route from the motel brought me back to Highway 202 from the day before. I found the portion that I would ride today to be much wider, with new paving and a good bike shoulder, another pleasant surprise. Weekend traffic was light, making for easy traveling. As I neared Conshohocken, a first-class bike trail followed the road. Cyclists could use either the bike trail or the bike lane on 202. The bike trail continued for about eight miles, using one side of the road or the other. Lots of locals were out riding, running or walking on a very pleasant morning.

Upon arrival in Conshohocken, my plan was to join the Adventure Cycling route and the Schuylkill River Trail. I followed the very busy trail for about 10 miles and then exited at Valley Forge, General George Washington's winter camp for the Continental Army. I had been there before but never on a bicycle. Most of the bike trails around the park must have been made for mountain goats, even though I am sure Washington viewed the hills as providing an advantage should his camp be attacked. When it was time to go, I made a huge blunder and turned the wrong way. After I had ridden for more than two miles, a local resident informed me where I had made my mistake. He was a great guy and even drove ahead to make sure the proper road was open despite a "Road Closed" sign for some weekday construction. Back on the right track and again climbing the same hills, I saw the resident ride back by with his thumb up and out the window. I knew I could make it through. I had spent too long at Valley Forge and then wasted time by being lost and climbing extra hills, so I had to make a decision on the fastest way to get back on track. Checking my state map, I realized I was in for a long day.

I chose to use Route 23 to Reamstown, where I could again join up with the Adventure Cycling route. I needed some major fuel and stopped for a large Mountain Dew and several Reese's Cups. I used this combination only when I was behind my planned pace and the result was likely to be significant hours of hard pedaling. I had to make up some time with more rolling hills ahead.

Why Mountain Dew and Reese's Cups when I get in a bind?

I don't know for sure, but the combination has certainly evolved into the best energy boost for a late day physical push. I don't drink soft drinks often when not on rides, and a Reese's cup package once a month is about the only time that I go for that treat. Being a personal trainer and a student of nutrition, I know that there are other choices for sustained energy. However, both of these items are readily available along the road, and when the drink is mixed with ice, I feel an immediate boost. Sure, most of it comes from caffeine and sugar, but I have averaged burning about 7,000 calories a day. For example, on this particular day, I was on the bike for about 13 hours. I needed to physically push well past the normal effort until I was safely in the motel just before dark.

The term "even a wild hog sometimes finds an acorn" seemed to fit me once again. Route 23 turned out to be one of the most beautiful roads I've ever cycled on, and that says a lot. Considering that I have now ridden through Maine, Montana, Oregon and Idaho, this was a spectacular ride. Heading mostly west out of Valley Forge on Route 23, I saw various Revolutionary-era homes and a cemetery for Continental Army soldiers. Eventually the scenery transitioned into Civil War-era homes and farms with well-kept yards and buildings. The road wasn't particularly hilly, and traffic was moderate.

There was more to come. Route 23 began a transition into Amish farmland, always some of the prettiest farmland around. Hay baling was in progress, just ahead of a threatening thunderstorm. I had a long way to go, but the beautiful scenery was a real plus. At a stop for food and cold water, I asked Jim Shankweiler of Elverson, Penn., whether I was on the right track. Jim and I talked about what I would see later, and he said that he would be visiting North Carolina soon. Jim assured me that I could make Reamstown by late afternoon.

Later in the day, I had several choices on how to make the final connection to Reamstown and a possible motel. I stopped at the huge grocery store in Goodville and got help from Bret and Cindy on how to make the shortest ride to meet my goal. They took time to print out a MapQuest list of directions and explained why this route was best. With the sun starting to set, I had about 10 miles to go.

What followed was another amazing experience. I rode through back roads of Amish farmland, marveling at seeing one farm after another up close. Kids played in the yards while milking continued in the dairy barns. Teens and young adults were out walking or riding bikes, and everyone waved as I passed. This one single experience was the best yet on my total ride. When a turn was left out of the MapQuest directions, I stopped at a house to ask for help. No one came to the door, but a young Amish woman was just then pushing her bicycle up the hill in front of the house. I walked over and got very clear directions from her as to how to find my destination. She smiled often as she cleared up the problem with the missing road.

After several visits over the years to the Amish farmland in multiple states, including some on both long-distance bike rides, I felt most comfortable here. As a kid, I was first exposed to milking cows on our own dairy farm. It was very small, and my dad usually did the milking before he went to his other job. Sometimes, and especially on weekends, my brother and I went along to help. By my mid-teens, the family had given up the dairy business. Yet just about everything about farm life evokes pleasant memories for me. I can remember the mad rush to get the hay into the barn before a thunderstorm hit and the thrill as a child of seeing the tractors and equipment do their work.

Today, as a part-time farmer, I still enjoy the best of that world. Physically, the work can sometimes be hard, but the rewards of seeing a clean hay field as the sun sets or as the rain starts to fall are special to me. Often my other work does not provide clear and immediate results. Farming helps me fill that void. My favorite time on the farm has remained the late afternoon after the work is done, when I can sit and watch the horses graze in a nearby pasture as yet another gorgeous sunset fades into dusk.

Following the discussion with the Amish lady, I was about three miles away from the town but no more certain about how to find the motel. I actually called and asked how to find it, but the desk clerk's mixed English directions didn't help much. Just then, I saw a woman in front of a nearby house. I rode over to her, and Jill gave me the best route to find the motel. Of course, I needed to ride the wrong way on a one-way road. I was glad to do it, and I finally pulled into a Red Carpet Inn that sat under a huge sign calling it the Red Roof Inn. I went to the desk and told the clerk that I had called a couple of times and had finally made it. With a few English words that I could understand, she asked for $12 more for the night than she had quoted me that morning. I reminded her, and she quickly changed back to the lesser price.

It had been a long day, covering 90 miles, but I had seen possibly the best scenery on the whole ride. Thinking back on the long climbs, the wrong turn and all the direction issues, I still called this the best overall day yet. I had lots to do before bed. I rode into the motel at 8:30 p.m., then still had to buy food, submit my story and photos, take a shower and do some planning for tomorrow. It was almost midnight by the time my head hit the pillow. After the actual ride has been finished for the day, I often had to complete all of these things in a timely manner. I had to transmit the story and photos back to the paper by certain deadlines, and on occasion my motel's Wi-Fi didn't cooperate. This was one of those nights and required a walk toward the office and a better connection to submit the final pieces. Eventually, it always got done, but I found it hard to wind down. The amazing part of all of this is that my normal routine had become something like 16-18 hours on the go and often only six hours of rest, and I did it almost every day and genuinely loved it.

Less than the aforementioned six hours later, I was up and had planned to leave by 6:30 a.m. I picked up my cellphone and realized it had not charged overnight, and then found that my iPad had not either. The Red Carpet Roof Inn had at least two outlets that didn't work. I needed both the phone and iPad to have a decent charge to make it through the day. Both were moved to other working outlets as I delayed checking out. My 8 a.m. departure turned out to match the latest for the whole ride, and I felt behind as I pulled away.

Rejoining the Adventure Cycling map was my goal, so I asked for the location of the proper road to start that route. A small benefit of the delay was seeing six Amish carriages as I rode through town. The passengers were all dressed well and on the way to church. I waved, and they returned my greeting. I realized that I just felt more comfortable riding on farm roads that had horse manure on them. Not many cyclists would say that, but I will admit to smiling just a little bit more when I see dried manure stretching out ahead of me.

Seeing the Amish up close like this makes me wonder whether I could live that life. A slower pace with lots of intrinsic rewards appeals to me greatly. On one hand, I love the thought of spending a month in New York City rushing here and there. But on the other hand, for true peace of mind, would anything be better than a simple life on one of these immaculate farms?

My first roads that morning headed out again through more of the Amish and Mennonite farms. Not a single person was around the farms, probably because everybody had gone to church. As the roads got hillier, I was joined by a small cycling group practicing for an upcoming ride in Iowa. We talked often as they leapfrogged me heading west. I last saw them practicing eating for Iowa later at a convenience store in Manheim. I said good-bye and headed out for Mt. Joy and more hills. It appeared now that Pennsylvania was trying to challenge Connecticut for the worst climbing.

The mighty Susquehanna River became my companion as I

headed through Marietta, Columbia and Wrightsville. I noticed that Wrightsville had been significantly involved in the Civil War, uncommon for this area. When a portion of Gen. Robert E. Lee's Confederate Army advanced to cross the bridge as part of the Gettysburg campaign, the Union army burned the bridge to stop them.

Leaving Wrightsville on a flat street felt great as another rider pulled up beside me. I could tell he was an experienced cyclist by the way he handled his bike. We talked a little about my ride, then he told me good-bye and to "enjoy the upcoming hills" as he rode away in another direction. Just what I needed for today after already being behind! The Susquehanna River was buried deep in a valley, and my route took me up and over the range of hills. Another hill somewhat similar to Bobby Sprocket's Woodbury, Conn., vertical climb rose above me, with plenty of vehicles passing by.

After reaching the top of the series of hills, I came upon the large Lake Clark and realized that this is where all the traffic was going. Hundreds of boats and plenty of people made this a big tourist spot. Surprisingly, there were no stores except for an outfitting service. Stopping at Shanks Mare Outfitters, I got some guidance from Brandon Ehrhart on what to expect as I climbed once again up and away from the lake. With sweat dripping off my elbows for the first time this summer, I had to stop for some ice cream just before leaving town.

On through Airville and Sunnyburn without much notice of a real town, I made it to Otter Creek and a beautiful campground. For the first time on the trip, I seriously considered spending the night camping in this area but decided to push on. Already I knew of at least one motel option in Delta, but first I had to get there. Late that Sunday afternoon, I began a long and grueling climb up and over the farmland in the area. Workers were actually baling some green hay as I passed over a picturesque ridge. Some of the farmland belonged to the Amish, even though I had more evidence than just horse manure on the roads. I spotted a carriage as they stopped to visit friends. In my previous book, I told about my learned knowledge of what major power lines mean when they cross hills or mountains ahead of me. This knowledge came in useful even in these Pennsylvania hills. I knew I had attained the highest point of my climb when I reached the major lines.

From that point on, I rode with moderate Sunday afternoon traffic for about 10 miles into Delta. An unusual roundabout, with not much nearby, was the first sign I was close. I called the motel and asked how much farther. His reply was sweet, "Only about a quarter mile, on the left!" I stopped at a convenience store for some food and quickly found the motel. According to the desk clerk, I had only a mile downhill to reach the Maryland line. That would come in the morning. Storms were closing in as I went to bed after 69 hard-fought miles. I felt great after another day of adventure.

Chapter 8
— Maryland
and District of Columbia —

Cycling south of the Mason-Dixon Line

After possibly the best night's sleep yet, I woke up excited about the upcoming day. The big storm overnight was loud enough to hear but not loud enough to keep me awake for more than a few seconds. People have often asked if I slept well while on these rides. The answer has been a resounding yes, possibly resulting from the fact that I finish necessary tasks before going to bed and don't leave things to do until the next morning. My mind has been clear and my body physically tired when my head hit the pillow. I have tried daily to keep up with responsibilities and returning messages, as well as any research that needed to be done on soon-to-be-traveled roads. The best sleep comes when I know that storms have been hitting the area while I am safely inside. More storms were in the forecast for the next few days, so I reasonably expected some additional restful sleep over the upcoming nights.

Within a couple of miles, I found the Maryland sign. Right beside it was the Mason-Dixon Line sign, signifying unofficially that I had made my way into the South. The actual Mason-Dixon Line was first used to settle a dispute in the mid-1700s about the borders of Maryland and Pennsylvania. Surveyors Mason and Dixon spent five years finalizing the actual border. During the Civil War, the Mason-Dixon Line signified roughly the dividing line between the North and the South. In 1902, the line was again surveyed and found to be remarkably correct. It still serves as the border between the two states.

Still following the Adventure Cycling maps, I used Highways 164 and 24, as well as a bunch of back roads on a humid morning. Low clouds and fog lingered from the overnight rain. There was more climbing but nothing extreme. The highlight of the morning was biking through a series of very large horse farms, many with old and stately homes.

I passed through the little village of Corbett, looking probably just about the same as it had appeared for the past 100 years. After briefly being lost because of incorrect distances on the maps, I met another cyclist named Dave who had a Surly bike and had ridden to Maryland from Portland, Ore. When I saw him, he was just 12 miles from home. Nothing else significant happened in the morning, and the afternoon brought a building threat of more storms. I stopped in Reistertown and replenished my food supply at a convenience store. It was great to see the first Food Lion grocery store, the chain that started near my home in Salisbury, N.C. After visiting some of the Hannaford stores farther north, I saw the similarities between them and Food Lion but now doubted that I would see any more Hannafords. That turned out to be correct.

After using gently rolling Highway 128, I knew that all roads didn't have to be as hilly as I headed south. The hills were definitely calming down as I neared Washington, D.C. I rode for a while on Ward's Chapel Road under a heavy downpour. About the time the rain started to lessen, I came to an intersection and spotted a pleasant looking man watching the rain and me riding by. I stopped to talk with Bobby Teague for a few minutes on the porch of his business. Bobby was from North Carolina and also is the brother of NASCAR race driver Brad Teague. Bobby still has his North Carolina accent, seemed a great guy, and I believe would have made a good neighbor. He asked me to sit down and join him, and while that offer was very appealing, I had to keep pedaling.

After a short break, another storm threatened, this time with some significant lightning. I didn't have a place to stay, or even any possibilities. Usually someone along the way would have some good information, and I hoped for more of the same with a stop at The Pink Cabbage, best described as an antique and other things shop. While I was in the shop, both Jackie Boulin and Michelle Rosata tried hard to give me some ideas but couldn't come up with any lodging possibilities anywhere close. While we talked, the thunder rumbled. I had to get going, but uncertainty was creeping in. The sky looked ready to explode as I went out the door.

Rain started within a few minutes, enough to make me turn on my flashing light and put on a rain coat. This one looked serious. I passed through Glenelg, where the heavy rain began. With my uncertainty building, it was on through Dayton and then to Brookeville. The Adventure Cycling map was confusing here, probably because lots of new road construction had occurred. Some of the mapped roads didn't seem to exist anymore. It was now 6:48 p.m. on a rainy night. I called the nearest bike shops, and they had no idea where I was. Adventure Cycling would send me toward a more rural area with no motels or even campgrounds. It was "seat of the pants" time again.

Often I get a charge out of the times on the road when no apparent answer exists toward a particular dilemma. This was one of those times. I had no perfect solution as to how to get to a good place to spend the night. If I followed the Adventure Cycling maps, there was nothing to do but ride until it was completely dark and then find a place to stealth camp. With more rain in the forecast, I didn't want to take a chance and end up spending a miserable night somewhere in this unfamiliar area.

I decided to take a more direct route toward Rockville, Md. Rockville was my goal anyway, but the choice was a regular four-lane road or a meandering ride around a big loop. A dad and daughter were cleaning up some storm damage along the road in Brookeville. The man was familiar with my new route and offered suggestions. I wanted to help them load some big tree limbs, but he said, "No, go on, you have a ways to go. We are going to drag the big stuff with the truck anyway." I headed out of town as fast as I could pedal.

Arriving in Rockville, I asked three people about motels. A motorist buying gas said that I had one choice: Ride west about five miles, and there would be some possibilities. I jumped back on my bike for another frenzied ride. It was almost dark, and I needed to find a place quickly. A Comfort Inn and a Red Roof Inn both were on my left, and I saw that the Comfort Inn didn't have outside access to the rooms. Quickly on to the Red Roof, I walked into the desk area amid a busload of Oriental kids. The first guy at the desk told me the motel was full, and I asked if there was anything else close by. His response was not positive, but by now I had learned that motel clerks won't tell much about other choices, even though he said that his rooms were booked solid. By now, it was nearly 9 p.m., and I had 90 miles completed. I went back to the desk, told them about my ride and asked whether they could find a room for me. The result was a large room, one of the best I had anywhere, though it was the only one that cost almost $100 total. Did I forget to say that they gave me the handicapped room? Both those guys ended up in my newspaper story about that day's ride, along with their photos. I admitted later to using the publicity for leverage to get them to dig a little deeper to find a room. Both of them perked up when I asked them for their complete names so that I could put their picture in my hometown paper along with the story. Let it rain—I was in the dry once again!

Out early again Tuesday morning, I was headed for Washington, D.C., by midday. Nearly every time that the late nights were the result of long rides, I told myself that I could wait a little later to leave the next morning. Not a single time did I do that. Every morning, I awoke with excitement about a new adventure. I would look at the clock and decide whether to stay in bed or get up to start the day. Always "starting the day" won out. I couldn't sleep when a new adventure was in the offing.

Many of the storms overnight had caused major damage in the area, according to early morning TV reports. The recent damage on other bike trails made me wary of what I might find today. One of my favorite terms is "There is nothing to do but do it." I left hoping that a morning scheduled for riding long urban trails would not present any major problems.

The day started slowly. A quick stop by the convenience store helped to reload my supplies before I headed for the Rock Creek Park Trail Head. Ted and Jane were out walking that morning and asked about my ride. I stopped riding to talk with them and realized how humid it was, especially after the late afternoon and overnight storms. Sweat started to roll off my upper body, and I knew it was time to start pedaling and generate a little breeze.

Rock Creek Park is a linear park, close to 15 miles long. Lots of cyclists, runners and walkers were on the trail, using various access points along the way. The entire trail was paved, though some of it was very rough. The signage was poorly done, but I had been warned about that. Every time I took the wrong turn, it didn't take long to figure it out. Spur trails just added to the confusion. Construction on certain segments did too. Rock Creek itself was well-kept and appealing as a park. When it ended, my map said that I should get on the Capital Trail. Not once did I see a sign for that trail, so possibly it had changed names since the map was printed. By asking Luther Perkins and Anita Jackson some specifics, I finally found the Potomac River. Washington, D.C., on this bright and sunny day was spectacular. I came off the trail near the Kennedy Center, then rode toward the Arlington Bridge. I could see the Washington Monument and the Lincoln and Jefferson Memorials, along with many statues. The bike trail along the Potomac was smooth and easy to ride. Lots of cyclists, walkers and runners were out using the trail around noon. One of my favorite parts of the trail passed under the landing path of Reagan International Airport. Those big jets seemed almost close enough to touch as they passed over, probably farther away than they appeared. A large crowd was taking this in, proving that even city folks can be amazed at times by simple things. Some even had picnic lunches, and quite a few large families had set up lawn chairs to enjoy the scene in comfort. I could have easily spent several hours here, admittedly often amused by simple things myself.

Another highlight was a long motorcade of official limousines that passed by as motorcycle police stopped traffic. The motorcade rushed by just before I pedaled onto the Mt. Vernon Trail. About 10 cars were in the motorcade, all similar in appearance and sporting government license plates. I tried to quickly get a picture, but only got the last car in line. This bike path followed the highway as it headed south. I never saw any signs for the District of Columbia, either entering or leaving. Regardless, I was now headed for Virginia.

From what I saw of Washington, D.C., it is another haven for cyclists and runners. Hundreds of both passed me in the short time that I rode through the area. The scenery for these fitness activities along the Potomac is appealing, to say the least. I made a mental note to return to Washington very soon to explore the museums and government buildings again and enjoy the running paths. My stay in this area was too brief.

Chapter 9
— Virginia —

History surrounds me,
plus some thoughts at halfway

After following the Mt. Vernon Bike Trail, and once in a while jumping on the less bumpy highway, I made it to Mt. Vernon. With lots of curves and quick up and downs, the bike trail was better suited for a mountain bike. I didn't plan to stop in for a tour because I had done that before. The hot and muggy afternoon continued, and storms clouds were rolling in. Just as I figured out how to head back over to US 1, a few bolts of lightning raced across the sky. A downpour was imminent, but I was ready. I had my rain jacket but not much room to ride. The rain started to fall heavily immediately, so heavy that I looked for shelter. I saw a building that was supposed to have been a Mt. Vernon stable at one time. The only vehicle around was leaving, so I rode over and stopped under a small overhang. It was a nice break and mostly dry, although some of the rain was blowing in. All I could do was lean against a wall, with no place to sit down. The rain poured for about 40 minutes and then significantly lessened so that I could safely put my bike back on the road.

On US 1, just past Fort Belvoir, traffic was extremely heavy, with no shoulder to the road at all. But since the traffic was moving slowly, the drivers didn't seem to mind much that I was riding with them. Eventually the rain stopped, and a bright sun came back out. I didn't expect it to stay out for long. More clouds were in the distance. Two brownies on sale at a 7-Eleven picked me up for the rest of the ride.

While on my bike rides, I have made independent studies of

motels and convenience stores. No one has contracted me for this research, but that is OK. I have been willing to do it for free. Convenience stores out west were often the center of small towns, sometimes even serving as the post office and providing other services. Usually, I preferred the smaller mom-and-pop convenience stores to the major chains. Small regional chains have actually been my favorites. Some of the pertinent data that has been considered includes the price and available flavors of ice-cream sandwiches, willingness to give free ice for water bottles and available seating inside when it was especially hot or rainy outside. Two more things mattered to me, probably more than to others. I needed pizza by the slice and pastries with late day discounts. Finally, the staff had to have pleasant attitudes. If the convenience store had all these things, then it rated high on my list.

On this trip, the national winner remained 7-Eleven, repeating from the cross-country ride. Prices have been consistently reasonable and most of the above criteria earned high marks. The regional winner is easily Kum and Go, meeting all of the criteria above. Kum and Go has locations in 11 states from Arkansas to Wyoming. Of course, all data has been recorded only in my own independent survey. Sadly, Kum and Go is not located on the East Coast. No obvious contenders were noted during the East Coast ride.

I followed US 1 to Dumfries and stopped to ask about a room at the Super 8. The price was good, and the location had several stores so that I could stock up on food. The next round of rain was building as I put the bike in my room, talked with the owner about my trip and then headed out to stock up. Just as I got back, the rain started to fall again. Storms continued throughout the night, and I totally enjoyed watching and listening to the rain. The motel room window would actually open, a pleasant surprise that I always appreciate. Total mileage for today was 67.

With today's ride, I was nearly halfway from Maine to Key West. It seemed like a good time to reminisce a little about the happenings so far. I had pedaled through New York City and Washington, D.C., and portions of 10 states and the District of Columbia. Bigger and longer states would now be the focus for the rest of the trip, though I have enjoyed passing through all of the ones so far. With a few thoughts on the states, I can leave that subject behind for the time being. So far, the most scenic states have been Maine and Pennsylvania. History abounds in both, and there is a wonderful environment to take in the scenery and history by bike. Most of the states have been clean, but there have been challenges. Massachusetts roads and streets are the worst, though they are significantly more challenging in the towns. Lots of streets have poor pavement and plenty of potholes. Rhode Island had the best roads that I saw, but I was only in that state for a couple of hours. Riding US 1 has been the most fun so far, partly because it is historic, passes through and by significant areas, and there are plenty of choices for motels and resupply.

New Jersey is the dirtiest state I have ever seen and needs significant attention. Connecticut is the hilliest, followed closely by New Hampshire, Pennsylvania and Maine. The difference in the hills from out West is that these hills require continued up and down pedaling. Out West, there are plateaus that allow for significant flatter stretches. You might spend a day climbing from 3,000 feet in elevation to 4,000 feet in elevation, but then it would level off before a gradual climb on up. These East Coast hills often required a 600-foot climb, then dropped down nearly as far, followed by a climb right back up again. This goes on, over and over, until the effort required is greater than I expected, and often even more challenging than higher elevations such as the Rockies and Cascades.

I have been on the road for more than two weeks, and I have now settled into a pattern of pushing hard during the day and trying to rest, eat and prepare in the evening. Most evenings, I don't make it to bed until about 10:30 and sometimes much later. Those midnight end-of-day prayers leave only five to six hours of sleep, which I know is not enough after a tough after a day of cycling. There will be plenty of time for additional rest after I conclude the ride in Key West.

My normal and very strict diet has once again gone out the door, most likely not to be seen again until the end of the ride. Things that I don't normally eat have been a part of my daily 7,000-calorie-plus gorging. Cinnamon buns (especially heated ones), cookies, plenty of Reese's Cups and caffeine-laced drinks are staples. I have eaten well from grocery stores when they are available, choosing lots of bananas, other fruit and Greek yogurts. I craved all of those things, especially big slabs of watermelon. Ice cream and Power bars remained a staple, and by now I know that these foods somehow combine to make my internal engine go.

At this point, I have felt great, with nothing hurt or sore. The bike seat doesn't bother me. My arms have become more tired than my legs; in fact, by the afternoon, especially on hilly days, I can barely raise my arms. The arm leverage required to keep pumping the legs takes a toll after a while. At the end of a long day's ride, walking usually felt a little awkward, and it can take a while for my arms to feel normal again, but everything comes back around overnight.

Some of my delights at the end of the day have included the endless eating, taking off my socks and shoes for the first time, putting my feet up on the bed, returning messages to those that have corresponded, a long shower, and finally the thankful prayer before going to sleep. Usually I have fallen asleep within a minute of my head hitting the pillow, a delight within itself.

All the states remaining are familiar to me, though I have never been to parts of each of them that are on my planned route. I have been looking forward to Key West, having never been south of Miami. The adventure continues!

Dumfries was a pleasant stop and is the gateway to the rest of a history-laden tour of this portion of Virginia. I was squarely in the middle of a Civil War hotbed, being surrounded closely by several major battlefields. Because of this, I planned to free-lance again today on my route by staying early in the day with US 1.

Just out of Dumfries, I came across the entrance to the United States Marines Museum. At 7 a.m., I knew they wouldn't be open yet, so visiting here will be on my list for later. My plans included a visit to historic Fredericksburg, site of a major Civil War battle and Revolutionary War happenings as well. I had passed through before but never spent any real time there.

Upon reaching Fredericksburg, what turned out to be a source of amusement was my first series of inquiries about where to find the major historical sites. I stopped at a convenience store and asked two clerks and a customer. None of them had any idea where the battle occurred or any idea about a visitor center. After spotting a sign that designated one turn as the way to downtown Fredericksburg, I took that street. Soon I was immersed in a beautiful old village that held its history so well. I kept pedaling and asked yet another person walking through town where to go for the battlefield and a possible visitor center. He said, "I don't know about the battlefield, but it is somewhere close by. There is a visitor center about one street over." Later, I realized that we were probably within sight of a portion of the battlefield while having the conversation. Having pedaled only 23 miles at this point, I still decided to take a trolley tour for a better understanding of the history of Fredericksburg. There was time to watch a brief video on how Fredericksburg came to be before the 90-minute tour, which turned out to be well worth the delay. These sightseeing tours have always been a great way to get a handle on the layout of an area and then position yourself for seeing more of your specific interests. The very helpful folks in the visitor center even watched my bike for me.

We learned about George Washington growing up across the Rappahannock River, near the staging area for the Union troops at the Civil War battle of Fredericksburg. Washington's mother lived here and the local college is named after her. Mid-1700s houses were everywhere, and most of them were in good repair as well as being quite expensive now. Most interesting to me was a visit to the Sunken Road, center of the battle where 18,000 casualties resulted from Union soldiers charging the Confederate Army high ground in 1862. The National Park Service has done a great job here. Fredericksburg reminded me of a smaller and more compressed Charleston, S.C. My time was well spent, but because I had stayed longer than planned, I decided to skip the Stonewall Jackson Memorial and head on toward Richmond. I promised to visit the memorial and other battlefields like the Wilderness, Spotsylvania Courthouse, Chancellorsville and Manassas on another trip. One person told me Jackson's arm could be seen at the house where it was amputated, but I was later informed that it was buried nearby.

A long climb from the riverfront eventually got me back on US 1, and in the vicinity of Interstate 93. I noticed that traffic was heavy, but that at every exit toward 93, many of the vehicles would leave us. That suited me just fine. With every vehicle that exited US 1, the traffic around me became less hectic.

I had read online about a motel that I wanted to call for a good deal that evening. After an enjoyable ride for most of the afternoon on good bike shoulders, I stopped at a McDonald's to use the bathroom and call the motel. My thought process still had me several miles from the motel, but I noticed a Food Lion nearby. After wondering if I would have a grocery store near my motel, I finally made the call. The owner asked me where I was, and I described the area. It turned out that I was about 300 feet from his motel, so I got my wish about having a good grocery store nearby and getting a great deal on a room. Yogurt, Power bars, watermelon, bananas and a protein shake filled my stomach that night. Total mileage today was 74 on a pleasantly cool and enlightening day.

My motel was on the northern outskirts of Richmond. I planned an early ride through the city as I hit the pillow that night.

My plan to ride through the middle of the city worked out even better than expected. The route of US 1 was easy to follow even though the signs called it different street names and seldom used the highway logo. Drivers and pedestrians were very laid back as I pedaled through town, even though I was riding during rush hour. During my time in New York City and New Jersey, fast driving and constant horns were the norm, and I certainly appreciated the difference probably dictated by the slower pace of the South. I never got a horn, and the drivers gave me plenty of room throughout.

My goal for the day was to make Suffolk, Va., on Highway 460. But first, I passed through Petersburg, yet another beautiful and historic city that could easily have kept me busy for another tour. Joining 460 was a bit of a challenge, but once again a wrong-way ride on a one-way street got me there. I wouldn't see US 1 again until Florida, but I looked forward to that time. After riding significant hills for the first half of the ride, I hoped to get a break soon, and with that thought, things changed.

Highway 460 took me into the coastal plain of Virginia. Almost 50 miles of straight road with only an occasional moderate hill was a wonderful gift. Usually, I had at least some shoulder, though the initial parts of the highway were crowded with trucks. Early on, the pavement was in poor shape as well. Both situations gradually improved until later in the day when the riding became much easier. I just put the pedal down and pushed on for 90 miles of uneventful riding. I rode through Virginia peanut country and passed through portions of swamp for the first time. As an oddity, I didn't get to meet any special people that day. As I have said before, meeting people makes the adventure. Moderate temperatures continued, though I had a suspicion that some hot days were not far away.

This was my last planned full day in Virginia. My estimation after reaching Suffolk was that I had pedaled about 1,400 miles and had about that much more to go. I had been blessed with good weather, no serious mechanical issues, and had met plenty of helpful and interesting people.

Once again, I planned to leave Suffolk with a specific route for the next day but got up and changed it. I wanted to visit another historic little town and see some water, so I chose to use Highway 32 to reach Plymouth in North Carolina. Rolling out of town, I found that Highway 32 was a good choice. Traffic was light, and I had plenty of room to ride. Larger sections of swamp dominated both sides of the road, and once I thought I spotted an alligator as it ran from me and dove in the water. George Washington had tried to drain a portion of the swamp with limited success.

About 8 a.m. that morning, and 12 miles south of Suffolk, I returned to North Carolina. It was a great feeling to be somewhat back home. This part of North Carolina was mostly new to me. I saw the first of many small family cemeteries. I was now in rural farmland with lots of cotton and soybeans. The air seemed fresher and the sky more blue.

My time spent in Virginia on both rides has been calming and has come at good times in the big picture of the whole journey. Virginia has good roads, pleasant people and is so similar to North Carolina that I enjoyed the state more than most others. It has been a real pleasure to visit Virginia by bike, and I have nothing but good memories.

Chapter 10
— North Carolina —

Back home, but only for a little while

Initially, I noticed that the North Carolina roadsides in this area were especially clean. I have no idea whether the homeowners made the extra effort, but I could see hardly any trash. When passing by on a bike at 12 mph, it is easy to spot trash. People have asked me often what I do to pass the time when there is nothing special to look at. I have replied, "There is always something to look at, but once in a while I enjoy looking at the trash beside the road." For example, out in the far western states, I was able to look at the different sizes of bungee cords and whether the hooks were still attached. In Maine, it was the liquor-by-the-drink bottles. In this part of North Carolina, there was almost nothing.

This is the area where I first noticed that my dependable bike was acting up. The chain was not shifting correctly and seemed to be occasionally skipping links. The terrain was tame, so this was not a big deal, but I knew it could be later on hillier sections. I could only try and figure out the problem at this point.

Traffic continued to be light, and it was a good morning for bike riding. I noticed a crop dusting plane ahead, climbing and diving over the fields next to the road. The plane continued its aerobatics as I drew closer, providing some great entertainment. Next came another gift when I rode onto new pavement. Nothing makes a loaded bike sing like new pavement. The effort required to pedal is less, the ride is better and usually a little faster, too.

On each ride, there are a few days when riding the bike is an absolute pleasure. I think it is what many people envision when they hear about what I do for fun. This particular day, especially enhanced by being in North Carolina, was starting out to be one of those good days. At this point, I was confident that I could find out the reason for the chain issue, and all the other factors were going well. Little traffic, plenty of easy scenery and excellent roads made this day seem just a little more special. I hoped for some people encounters to add an additional boost.

Paving worker Clifton was holding the stop sign out for traffic when I rode toward him, just inside the new pavement. I asked Clifton, who was now smiling, if I had to stop. His reply was, "No, but all these cars have to. You can go ahead, but don't hit anything." That was a much different reply than the one that started my confrontation with a paving company just a year before in the Grand Tetons. That group tried unsuccessfully to keep me from pedaling over a mile stretch when paving was in progress. They should have responded just like Clifton did.

To briefly recap the Wyoming paving saga of July 2013, I had ridden in heavy traffic through Yellowstone Park and on into the Grand Tetons. Signs for paving were posted on a Sunday afternoon during Fourth of July week, and all of that had seemed very odd to me. Vacation traffic was stopped for up to 30 minutes at a time, and most of the motorists were understandably steamed about it. When it was finally my time to proceed ahead, I was stopped by one of the paving workers and told that bikes could not pass through the area. I was then told that I had to put my bike on the back of one of their trucks and let them carry me through the one-mile stretch to the other end, and at that point I could resume my ride.

Of course, I couldn't do that. Just one mile of riding in a truck in Wyoming would negate the cross-country ride, and I passionately expressed that to the various supervisors called to the scene. After most of an hour, they finally relented and let me ride the one mile on my bike, but only after I told them that they would have to stop me physically from doing it. It was the most challenging mile of 4,164 that made up the complete ride.

Getting a little hungry, I stopped at a convenience store out in the country. Two egg, cheese and tomato sandwiches looked like they would do the job, so I ordered them. James Cullins had cycled to the store to get gas for his mower and asked about my ride. He knew quite a bit about the area and volunteered information about what I would see later. Then he got on his bike and pedaled down the road holding a full can of gas, probably a much better rider than me.

The sign for Hertford reminded me of one of my favorite baseball players, Jim "Catfish" Hunter of the A's and then the Yankees. Hunter lost his life after a battle with ALS, or Lou Gehrig's disease.

Edenton was the biggest town of the day, and I hoped it might have a bike shop. I didn't come across one, so I pedaled on with the chain and shifting issue getting worse. Once in a while the chain would jump links and then lock up. I had to pedal backwards a couple of rounds in hopes that the chain would start working again. Some ice cream at McDonald's was all I got in Edenton, but it hit the spot.

One of the reasons I changed my route early this morning was to cross a big body of water shown on the maps. Suddenly I saw the Albemarle Sound and a long bridge. For most of the morning, I had a gentle tailwind, but when I climbed onto the bridge, a fierce left-shoulder headwind hit me hard. Pedaling got tougher immediately as I climbed up higher on the bridge. There was a bike lane that should have been ample, but the headwind kept propelling me toward the concrete barrier at the edge of the bridge. Gusts pushed me uncomfortably close to the barrier, which was less than knee high. Even though there was some traffic, I crossed to the other side of the bridge to lessen the danger of losing my balance because of the wind. After what seemed like a half hour, I came down off the bridge, and once again the wind moved in as a gentle tailwind.

That tailwind helped my focus as I headed toward Plymouth.

Lots of people were out in the yards along the way, and most waved back with a friendly smile. With 10 miles to go, my map disagreed with the road sign. I stopped to ask a crew painting the steep roof on the Pleasant Grove Methodist Church for help in choosing the best route. Tyler Reed, Robby Wright and David Oliver all came out and posed for pictures, and they told me that either way would work but advised that I stick to my planned route. It was about a mile shorter.

The last portion of the ride went well, even though I stopped to watch a watermelon harvest going on. Farm workers were lobbing watermelons up through the open windows of an old school bus where others were stacking them in crates. The workers were so smooth and quick that I had a hard time getting a photo of the melons in the air.

I rode into Plymouth and immediately pedaled toward the downtown waterfront area. I asked a motorist where my planned motel was, and he told me not to stay there. That unusual response was a surprise until he said, "It used to be a nice place, but it isn't now. There is another one on down the same road." I pondered that new information and decided to check out the first one anyway. I knew the price was right and as often has been said, "You are only going to be there to sleep for a few hours." I decided to stay at the first one after the owner showed me the room and it seemed OK. I saw that there was no soap in the room and there was not an ice machine in sight. She took care of both things by giving me ice and soap from the office and told me that the grocery was just about a mile away.

After getting the motel room and its good price, I headed back uptown to the Roanoke River waterfront. Plymouth has a lot of history, especially from the Civil War. The Confederate Army recorded its last land-battle victory here, and the Confederate Ironclad CSS Albemarle was sunk while moored here. I also saw the lighthouse for the river and got pictures of everything before heading back to the grocery store for evening food. The bike continued to get worse, even though I was happy with a solid 90 miles for the day.

The special day that I had hoped for had come true, except that I did not yet have a handle on what was necessary to keep the bike running right. I was almost sure that the chain was stretched, but I could not fix that myself. I decided to visit the first available bike shop and get some professional help.

Saturday morning, July 19, started with that same bike issue on my mind. As I left the motel, I realized the chain slipped or stopped turning every time it was under a strain. Once in a while there was some popping too. I still hoped that I could find the reason for the problem and fix it. I eased out of Plymouth and rolled through the first 20 flat miles without incident. More dogs were out than cars on that early morning, and the riding was easy. I rode through Pinetown and didn't see a person moving.

Next came Bath, the oldest town in North Carolina. I had never been to Bath and looked forward to taking a little time to explore the pretty little town and the home of pirate legend Blackbeard. Dozens of historical markers were at the site of the oldest house, the first library, the oldest church and so on. I enjoyed a stop at the visitor center and its exhibit on Blackbeard and pirate times in Bath. One unusual occurrence at the visitor center took me by surprise. I met and talked with the female attendant for a few minutes. I thought that she would make a nice photo for the paper and asked her to do that. She responded very politely, "Oh, no, I never allow anyone to take my picture. Thanks for the offer but I just can't." She would have made a very nice picture too. This was only the second time during both rides that someone didn't want a picture taken, and the other guy relented when told that it was for a newspaper article.

I knew the schedule for the North Carolina State Ferry to Aurora and soon headed that way, a short ride from Bath. While waiting for the ferry, I searched online for the nearest bike shop. Flythe's

Bike Shop in New Bern was my best bet, and I called them and described the problem. We decided that I should head that way as soon as I got off the ferry. In the meantime, I settled in for a nice ride during which I met several couples from the area. One family had brought some friends to ride across to Aurora and then ride back to the other side. I could easily have done that too if I hadn't had a bigger agenda.

The ferry was over 35 miles away from New Bern, and it was going to be a battle to get there with the way the bike was acting. "Nothing to do, but do it" came to mind, and as soon as I got off the ferry, the push was on for New Bern. I had enjoyed the ferry ride, but the bike's repair was on my mind even while talking with the local residents. Departing the ferry just before 1 p.m., I began the long, hard ride. I knew the bike shop closed on Saturday at 5:30 p.m., so I had to push hard to give them any chance to fix the bike by closing time. Since straining the bike seemed to cause the problem, I said a prayer for help to keep going. Only a couple of brief bathroom stops and a couple of cookies and some water got me off the bike between Aurora and New Bern.

I was confused at one corner, and just as I started to scratch my head about which way to go, a traffic angel named Brittany stopped to tell me about a shortcut to New Bern. She gave me her phone number for emergency help, and off I went, reaching the bike shop at 5 p.m. I felt as if I had just ridden a segment of the Tour de France.

Flythe's was a busy bike shop, and the very competent trio of Steve, Mac and Shawn went to work on the bike. Turned out that all the climbing earlier in the ride had worn down the big drive gears so much that they had to be replaced. Flythe's didn't have the exact replacement part for the Surly Long Haul Trucker, but they did have a set of Shimano crank and gears that would do the job. They changed it all out and took a link out of the chain, put on a pair of replacement pedals and did a quick tune up. I enjoyed the time with these great guys as they steadily fixed my bike. About 6 p.m., 30 minutes after they usually closed, I waved goodbye and headed back down the street. It was too late to get any photos of New Bern, but I planned to return another time.

Between the time of my first visit and the writing of this book, I have visited Flythe's Bike Shop again for additional information on yet another book, possibly titled "Cycling Coastal North Carolina." New Bern has lots to offer cyclists and tourists alike. More information on the remarkable history of one of the oldest bike shops in the state will be included in the possible 2016 release.

On to Pollocksville and my lodging for the night. I rode on Martin Luther King Boulevard, which then became Highway 17 South. There was a brief patch of new paving that included significant rumble strips, the only thing marring the very pleasant ride. It had been a long day as I pulled into the Trent Motel, a more than unique place. The only motel around, it took them about 20 minutes to check me in. A few of the things in the room didn't work, but that was OK. I asked about the nearest store and was told that it was just 300 feet up the road. Those 300 feet turned out to be slightly more than a half mile. Tired out from the long and hard push for the bike shop, I just picked up my food and headed back to make my report and get some needed rest. My Wi-Fi wouldn't work in the room, so I sat next to the office in the dark to send in my daily newspaper report. After a quick shower, I went to bed while the overhead ceiling fan shook dramatically. I only hoped it would stay attached to the ceiling for the rest of the night.

I hoped to be up early the next morning but overslept a little because my usual internal alarm didn't go off. My swanky abode had nothing to do with it, but I was out the door at 8 a.m. instead of the usual 6:30. The bike rode and shifted so well today that I made up time and soon joined Highway 17 heading for the coastal areas. Fresh paving added to my speed, and I started to feel great, probably influenced by the smooth ride. Lots of folks have asked me about being on that bike seat for so many hours a day. A good seat has been the key, but smooth riding on new pavement remained an extra gift.

My first towns were Maysville and Belgrade and next came busy Jacksonville, home of the Marine Corps Base Camp Lejeune. Many of the businesses were geared toward the young Marines. Cellphone stores, car lots with Jeeps, motels and practically every other business had banners advertising military discounts. I crossed the New River near Jacksonville and continued on toward Dixon and Sneads Ferry. Pedaling directly east took me to the Intracoastal Waterway and then Topsail Beach, just one more beach where one of my ex-wives used to have a home. Topsail is beautiful, with wide bike lanes, new paving and almost no stores, along with a wide variety of beach homes.

During my morning ride, I had thought this afternoon might be a good time to get off the bike early. I was ahead of schedule, and my mind needed a break. Some of my overused muscles probably cheered when I pulled off to get a room at the Loggerhead Motel in Surf City. Total mileage so far was 58 when I called it a day at 2 p.m. Although this was a coastal ride, I had not dipped my feet in the ocean yet. I took time to do it this afternoon, as well as walking some on the beach. Later, storms threatened but no rain fell as I enjoyed a good night's sleep again.

Time for another adventure, I was up earlier than usual and on the road even before dawn. There was some light rain, but it was so warm and humid I didn't even think of wearing my rain jacket. I took Highway 210 out of Surf City, and then joined Highway 17 again on the way toward Wilmington. Moderate traffic gradually increased during rush hour as I neared Wilmington. Good shoulders and courteous drivers helped get today's ride off to a positive start. After reaching the city, I hopped on Highways 132 and then 421 toward Carolina Beach. Carolina Beach was a favorite vacation spot for my family while the kids were small, and I played in softball tournaments here. Over the years, Carolina Beach has changed dramatically, with many choices for restaurants, stores of every kind and just about anything else available now. Hap Alexander from Salisbury sent me a message to stop and get a free breakfast on him, but I had to keep pushing.

My goal was the Fort Fisher Ferry and making the 10:45 a.m. departure. Earlier, I thought there was no chance, but then I saw that the Fort Fisher State Park itself was not open on Mondays. I had planned to spend some time at the fort itself, especially after recently reading a book about the defeat of the fort and the loss of the last significant southern port available for supplying the Confederate armies during the Civil War. Some quick figuring told me that I could barely make the ferry with a sprint for the last couple of miles. I made it with probably 30 seconds to spare and pushed the bike onto the ferry just as they closed the ramp. The quick sprint saved me another 45 minutes of waiting for the next one, but this time the ride was not free. The rain stopped as we made the crossing. I remember a bunch of tourists throwing bread crumbs to the sea gulls until one of the tourists got hit with a dropping. It was amazing how that pastime was not as much fun anymore.

After exiting the ferry at Southport, I rode through another historic town and realized that Southport was bigger than it seemed when traveling by car. Lots of trendy shops and plenty to see and do kept the visitors busy. Nowhere did I notice a sign announcing that yet another of my ex-wives had lived here. Surprised at that, I headed out of town with a smile on busy Highway 211 toward Supply, another long straight road with not much to look at. I began to mentally look forward to rejoining Highway 17 and more scenery.

My good friend and fellow cyclist Dwight Howell was vacationing at Ocean Isle nearby, and he knew I was passing through. We missed each other on phone calls and didn't get a chance to visit except by phone. My plan now was to push on toward Little River and get a room because rain again looked imminent. I got a great gift just before the South Carolina line as I was pedaling up a small hill. Friends from home, Bobby, Chris and Keaton Sloop, were waiting for me beside the road. They woke me up from my pedaling in the "end of the day daze," and we had a nice visit. What a boost near the end of the North Carolina segment!

Rain started to fall again as I came to the South Carolina line. My motel was just a few miles farther, and so was the last of my ride for the day.

Chapter 11
— South Carolina —

Heading inland, away from the beaches

At the end of the day, just after crossing the South Carolina line, I headed into Little River in the moderate rain. I had called the Lake Shore Motel the night before, hoping for a place right on my route. Just as I entered Little River, I called again to make sure they still had a room for me. Making reservations was always taking a chance, and the motel demand was not high in most small towns. That policy has worked well for both long rides. They did have a room, and it was one of the best yet. The room was what they called a single room, a little smaller than the others but fine for me and the bike. There was a nice little lake in front of the motel, one that had rain drops falling in it just about all night. No matter, rain and sleep always have gone well together for me. Total distance for this day was a relatively easy 94 miles. On this day, 94 miles was considered easy, but very soon a day with similar mileage would be one of my hardest.

Although my time at the Lake Shore Motel was brief, I realized that there are still some very good American family-owned motels. I had heard that all along the coast, few Americans still owned the small motels. I had formed an opinion on this after spending more than 20 nights in various motels along the Eastern Seaboard. The high standard still existed for some of the small owners, but for others it did not. The little extras that a reasonable place should have were gradually disappearing. Yet I think that some owners have held the line and will continue to do so. Quite a few times, I would enter a room and find something that didn't work. Light bulbs were missing or burned out. Soap was not available in the room without asking. There was a charge for ice, or no ice was available. As I said before, at one motel I was even charged extra for the use of the remote.

With that said, the nightly cost for many of the motels has come down, and competition appears to be the major factor. Some motels use the same rooms for smoking and non-smoking customers. The smell doesn't leave just because someone has removed the ash trays before check-in.

It was a real pleasure to stay in the Lake Shore Motel in Little River. I suggest that if you happen to need a room in that area, go see them. Everything worked well; the room was bright, all of the above and more were included, and the owner was not behind glass. She was very personable as well. This was not the only motel that had everything going right, but those good ones are in the minority.

When my internal alarm went off, I saw a moderately heavy fog and wondered if I should go out at the normal time or delay my departure. The decision, of course, was "go early, and things will work out," just as they did with only a minor delay for confirming directions. My red flashing light looked good as I would eventually ride toward Monck's Corner and Walterboro. By my calculations, there were still almost 1,100 miles to Key West, well over 650 in Florida alone.

Most of the towns I planned to see today were new to me, but I didn't expect any problems. First up was Wampee on Highway 90, and I never knew exactly when I got there. Just past Wampee, I rode up to a Wendy's offering breakfast and decided to give it a try. I learned from Keith Tedder that I could get an egg, cheese and tomato Panini as a regular item, no special order needed. That Panini was one of the best things I had ever tasted for breakfast, so I planned to get more on down the road. In fact, I thought about going right back in and getting a couple more for later in the day. I didn't, but should have.

The fog was just about gone as I pulled away from breakfast, hoping to turn on to Highway 31. The big road-closed sign announcing "Bridge Out, Four miles ahead" made me wary of possibly having to waste 8 miles of riding. I chose another route, Highway 90, which would also get me to Conway. Almost as soon as I got going, the dreaded rumble strips appeared. Plenty of trucks and other traffic were on this road, possibly with some of them taking Highway 90 for the same reason that I was. The next 14 miles were a little shaky as the big trucks moved over to go around me. I remember getting upset when several of them seemed to just miss me as they passed.

I rode into Conway, a much prettier town than it appears to be when we North Carolinians pass through on the way to Myrtle Beach. I asked a policeman about my road choices and the best way to Highway 701. He assured me I could just keep going the way I was headed. After a little too much northbound riding with no turn in sight, I stopped at a convenience store to get back on track. I had to retrace my route a bit and then head west, eventually putting me on the worst road of my whole journey. Highway 701 was loaded with trucks, and with the summer heat, those trucks had caused ruts and cracks in the pavement. Sometimes, I had trouble finding a flat place to ride, especially since the shoulders were very limited. More memories of my final miles toward Myrtle Beach last summer came to mind as I thought of having to endure too much traffic and poor roads for the last 50 miles of that cross-country journey.

I kept looking for Bucksport, which turned out to be nothing resembling a town. Next up was the similar Yauhannah. Signs offered deer and fish processing, but the smell made me think that the carcasses must be tossed near the road as a part of that process. After biking across about 25 states, I had never seen so many pieces of deer or dead fish beside the road. Just a little farther down the road was Pleasant Hill, the site of a good convenience store and little else.

The traffic had thinned somewhat as a rain shower fell, lasting only about 15 minutes. Just another cooling off shower. I passed through Rhems and never saw a town. Next came Highway 41 and more rumble strips, but even less traffic and fewer trucks. I headed into Andrews and immediately noticed that this was the hometown of Chubby Checker. For some happy reason, I started singing, "Let's twist again, like we did last summer …"

First stop was the post office to ship some things back home. Just as I did last year in Kansas, it was time to send back some unneeded items. Once again, I never used the bike lock, and there were maps and other paperwork that wouldn't be used again, either. I sent home nearly four pounds of stuff, which doesn't sound too big, but that total represented more than 10 percent of my non-food and drink weight. Every little bit helped when space could be made for extra water, too.

Andrews was a perfect place to spend the night. I made my way immediately to the Piggly Wiggly grocery store for some watermelon and yogurt, bananas and a few other items. My maps had already told me that a motel was close by and on the route. As the day came to an end, more twisting music came to my head. I used singing to pass the long hours on the bike last year, but those classic tunes like "Eastbound and down, loaded up and truckin', we're going do what they say can't be done" had not been replaced. I enjoyed having Chubby's music on my mind again. Music is good for the soul.

I got a real treat. The motel was a good one, again at a great price, and the owner gave me a quiet room with only a few cars passing by on the street. My Wi-Fi didn't work well in the room, but it was perfect out in the shade just in front of my door. I sat there watching traffic, typing away, eating a little watermelon and singing. What else could I want? It had been a good day, with 84 more miles.

Andrews had once been dubbed the fastest growing city in

the United States in the heyday of the railroad in the 1920s. That growth stopped shortly after, but the town seemed to be doing OK. I enjoyed my time in Andrews. People seemed upbeat, and nearly everyone greeted me when I passed them. Had I wanted to take a rest day, Andrews would have been a good place to do it. Those Piggly Wiggly grocery stores are small, but they had all of the staples that I needed. Many of the small South Carolina towns had booming Piggly Wiggly stores.

Even with no rain overnight, the fog had returned with the early morning of Wednesday, July 24. Once again, I headed south on Highway 41. I could see from my motel room that few vehicles were on the road. Right away, there were choices. Adventure Cycling wanted me to continue on toward some more very small towns with little scenery that probably formed the safer route. However, I was ready to wing it and see some people and scenery again. It has always been more fun riding with more than trees and poor roads to see.

I picked a route that included turning on US 17A and seeing some real towns. Right away, that choice looked like a bad one. The absence of road shoulders, with plenty of wide trucks squeezing past me on the pavement, made for a tight fit, but this didn't last for long. The traffic never built to anything past what I considered moderate. US 17A also alternated between sections of good pavement and sections of poor pavement. I suspected that the paving was contracted in different intervals, paved at different times. I rode through Jamestown and Macedonia, the latter hard to notice even on a bike. Some portions of paving had so many broken places that the bone jarring bumps couldn't all be avoided.

Just before Monck's Corner, I had a section of wide shoulders that was a wonderful break from riding next to traffic. As I entered the town, I noticed a Wendy's and planned to stop for another Panini. I found the door locked, with no breakfast being served. A banana and water had to do, and on I pedaled to McDonald's on the other side of town.

Summerville was the next town, a little bigger than most of the others. Summerville was originally called Pineland and was one of the first towns to enforce a tree law that fined residents for cutting them down. Summerville got its start during the Revolutionary War and still was loaded with many historic homes and a beautiful downtown area. Lots of friendly people waved, and Lou Melfi stopped to help me decipher the roads as I left town. Summerville is on my list to see again, partly for an explanation of why it was the first town to serve sweet tea.

Another unusual thing was a 16-mile sidewalk that ran between Monck's Corner and Summerville. New, straight and well done, the sidewalk was impressive. It also ran right beside generous bike lanes, extremely unusual in South Carolina. One more thing usually occurred while riding in the Palmetto State. If the road was good, I had better appreciate the moment because it wasn't going to last long.

The good road for the 16-mile stretch turned quickly to the worst road of the day as I headed to Cottageville. Lots of broken pavement and the most logging trucks that I had encountered since Oregon kept me on my toes. Dozens of logging trucks were passing me, going loaded one way and then returning empty for another load. Some were distinct in their appearance, and I realized the same ones usually came too close to me, occasionally prompting an outburst of less than nice words.

The road reminded me of Colorado last summer because the pavement was so bad that I couldn't avoid bumping over the bad places, not fun on a loaded bike. Colorado had little traffic, but this road sure had plenty. A brief but heavy rain made matters worse for a little while. This was the last time that I wore my Tyvek rain jacket—not because there was no more rain but because I must have let the jacket blow off the back of the bike while drying it. It was never seen again, though I had no idea where it was lost.

I rejoiced upon my arrival in Walterboro because the road improved a little, and I knew the end of this day was approaching. With no prior knowledge about lodging possibilities, I asked about motels. Several sources told that there was a big supply, simply because Walterboro is located along Interstate 95. What those sources differed on was the best one. One lady in a store told me to take one near the Waffle House in town, another said to go to the one near the Pizza Hut, and the most vocal said, "Go to the Rice Planter's Inn. It is very nice and only about $35. Come on and let's put the bike in the truck and I will take you there." I quickly told him that my code required that I ride the whole way. That price sounded too cheap for a clean place anyway. I had been told often before by people in the same town what a motel would cost. When I reached the motel, the previously quoted price was more than a few years old.

So with directions to the motel near the Pizza Hut and also the Rice Planter's Inn, I headed off down the road. Another pleasant surprise happened almost instantly. I saw a sign about the monument to the Tuskegee Airmen of World War II fame. The monument and some other history involved the Walterboro airport, so I rode that way. I found out that the airport was one of the biggest training facilities for pilots about to go to the war, and that the Tuskegee Airmen trained there as well. It felt good to be amid history again.

Back on the road into town and toward the motels, I saw a long sequence of beautiful moss-lined streets with plenty of historic homes on both sides. I stopped at another Piggly Wiggly and again saw one of the guys who had already given me directions. Amazing to me is how I commonly find the same person twice in a town that I have never been to before. That was about to happen again. Heading off to find the best motel, I stopped again to make sure I was on track and was told that the Rice Planter's Inn was just 4 miles ahead. By that time, 4 miles seemed a long way. But in yet another huge coincidence, the vocal resident who had told me about the Rice Planter's Inn was standing by the road at a gas station. He hollered, "It's just up there, on the left!"

I pulled in and found that the huge sign next to the interstate confirmed the great price. The motel looked fantastic from the outside. I had become pretty good at gauging the condition of a motel from the outside, especially after three weeks of riding on the East Coast. My thoughts were confirmed with a very courteous desk clerk, no window between us, and one of the better rooms that I had found anywhere. The clerk told me that breakfast at the Waffle House was included, and I could get it anytime. How could I beat that deal? To be honest, I never did.

It was a pleasure to get off the bike after 91 of the bumpiest miles yet and have so many choices around to get more food. What South Carolina lacked in roads, it made up for in good motels and nice people. This was one of the hottest nights of the trip, but I never knew it as I slept away another restful night. It was a real pleasure to get off the bike, kick off the socks and shoes, put my feet up and eat a little ice cream, watermelon and just about anything not nailed down while enjoying the air conditioning.

I had several goals in mind for the next day as I rose early again. During this stretch of a few days, I had some success getting on the road even earlier than usual due to the lack of traffic at that time. I was back on the Adventure Cycling map for the day, with goals of finishing map #5, reaching Georgia and also reaching Statesboro by day's end. To do this required close to 100 miles on a day that was predicted to hit near 100 degrees. More questionable roads were on the horizon as well.

The long day started with another journey on Highway 17A. I passed through Yemassee and headed toward Pocotaglio. This little town was right beside Interstate 95 and made up of motels and food places, all of them very reasonably priced. I didn't stop again but continued on to ride 4 miles on a service road beside the interstate. I passed a huge motel that had recently been closed down, noting that the price on the sign was well below the usual rates for that chain. There were some fantastic motel prices in this area of South Carolina.

This one day probably had the least traffic of the whole trip; never once was it an issue. That was great with me because it was also going to be the hottest day. A headwind developed that kept me cooler but also made pedaling harder. Gillisonville, Pineland and Robertville all passed by with little of note, most of it on Highway 462.

One memorable stop on this day was at the Garrett Post Office. I was a little unsure about the road, and it looked like a discrepancy had developed with Adventure Cycling maps. I noticed a pleasant looking man unlocking the door, and I stopped to get some information from Robbie Williams. Robbie and I talked about my ride, his cycling, what to expect through the rest of South Carolina, and finally where I could find a store on this hot day. He sent me off with a smile and lots of good information toward the little store in town, and then the Savannah River Bridge and the Georgia line on Highway 119. Robbie told me about the big hill that I would have to climb to get over the bridge, but honestly that bridge and big hill were a pleasant interlude and not too hard at all. No "Welcome to Georgia" sign was in sight, but I now had just two more states to go.

Chapter 12
— Georgia —

Hot temperatures and terrible roads

Now late in the day, I was in Georgia and wanted to reach Statesboro by nightfall. I had just crossed the Savannah River. I made a right turn onto Clyo-Kildaire Road, named for the towns on both ends of it. The temperature was rising, and the terrain became hillier than what I had ridden in the last couple of days. With a few more hills and a headwind, I also found new pavement. With every bad thing, I have found that there is usually a good one, too. I found this to be the case several times throughout Georgia.

The last 25 miles seemed to go on forever, but finally I saw Statesboro come into view after 99.5 miles for the day. The heat index was between 105 and 110, and that fact made this possibly the toughest day of the whole ride. I drank my fluids all day but spent significant time rehydrating some more that night. A trip to a nice grocery store and a wide-open AC unit in the room helped me get ready for more of the same the next day.

One strange occurrence that evening was worth mentioning. I chose one of several motels in the downtown area and went to the desk to see if I could check out the room first. The owner's wife was at the desk. She gave me the key, and I went to see the room. It looked great, so I turned the air conditioning unit on and went back to the desk to pay. She gave me a form to fill out; I paid and went back to the room. After my food run, I called the desk to ask if there was an ice machine. Her husband answered the phone and said, "We don't have anybody in room 112—how did you get in there?" I told him I had paid at the desk about 90 minutes before. He still didn't believe me and asked that I open the door so he could see which room I was calling from. Of course, it was room 112, and I reminded him again that I had paid his wife. He said, "I will have to check into this." I didn't hear from him again. They did have a huge ice machine, big enough to fill up coolers.

Out early again, expecting returning heat, I rode past Georgia Southern University on the way out of town. I decided to change back to a free-lance plan and ride a route that should set me up for ending the day before the heat got close to 100 again. With the right progress, I hoped to enter northern Florida tomorrow. I left Statesboro on Highway 25, a nice four-lane road with wide shoulders. A few challenging hills that came just south of Statesboro convinced me that the bike repair in New Bern had been the only option. The skipping chain would not have climbed these hills, so I rode south happily. A very reputable tourist later told me that the hills were the remnants of where the beach dunes used to be thousands of years ago. A few rumble strips occasionally got in my way, but never for very long.

I saw the signs for Claxton, Ga., coming up and thought of all the jokes that I have told over the years about fruitcake. Other and much better comedians have made even more fun of them, so I planned to ride over to the see if there was a brick and mortar distribution center and bakery. To my surprise, people do work at the Claxton Fruit Cake Company, and cakes were being baked and loaded on trucks. I had always thought that the same six fruitcakes were just passed around the world and nobody ever ended up with one for long. On the way out of town, I noticed another competing fruitcake company. Who knew?

With the heat building quickly in the morning, I made my second stop at a McDonald's for ice and this time for ice cream, too. Logging trucks were less of an issue today, so I didn't worry about traffic much. Early in the afternoon, I rode into Ludowici. Several roads came together there, and all the vehicles seemed to be going the same way as me. Suddenly, I was squarely in the middle of the heaviest traffic of the last few days. After a quick stop for a major refueling with Reese's Cups and cold Mountain Dew, I felt prepared to push on to Jesup and an early end of my ride for the day.

I was especially appreciative of the chocolate and the caffeine because it seemed that my final turn toward Jesup had put me on a road similar to an interstate. The heat continued to rise, but the breeze off the vehicles helped somewhat with that. With just about 11 miles to go, I was still confident of an early end to the day.

Out on a long bridge over a swampy area, I was concentrating on watching for nails and other sharp objects that could cause tire problems. With about seven miles remaining, I heard a clack, clack, clack coming from the back fender and immediately knew I had a problem. A mid-sized nail had stuck in the tire, just above the flat spot that rides on the pavement. From that point on, the day became a huge challenge.

I had about eight feet of breakdown lane to work on the tire. Everything was concrete; there were no soft spots or any shade, either. Repair of a back tire requires a lot of work, so I unloaded all my gear and started pulling out my tools and replacement tube. I slipped the rear rim off the bike, took the tire off the rim and then pulled out the damaged tube. With the heavy volume of traffic flying by, I wondered if anybody would stop. The heat and heavy traffic made it doubtful, but I was slowly making progress. I installed the new tube, replaced a tube liner that helps deter sharp objects from deflating the tires, and then put the tire back on the rim. So far, so good! I was sweating profusely as I prepared to inflate the tire. I usually do that with a CO_2 cartridge, one of the best things known to cyclists. I pulled out a cartridge and looked for the little connector that allows the cartridge to connect with the valve stem. I tore my bags apart only to realize that the connector was gone. Just about that time, the wind from a big tractor-trailer blew my favorite Dri-FIT cap off into the swamp below the bridge. What else was going to happen?

My only option was to use a very small emergency air pump, hope it would make connection and then pump it 500 times to get an acceptable air pressure in the tire. After getting about 70 pounds of air in the tire, I reloaded the bike, took one more look down into the swampy water and said goodbye to my hat, then started cautiously pedaling away. Just seven miles to go, although I was relegated to a slow pace so as to not put extra stress on the marginally inflated rear tire. Watching for more nails, I pedaled on and finally reached the outskirts of Jesup. I needed to get more air in that tire, something near 100 psi, or otherwise I doubted seriously that it would last much longer. One stop at an ATV place and another at an auto tire dealer netted nothing.

I had unhooked the rear brake to make replacing the back tire easier and had not hooked it back. When I saw the tire place coming up on the right, I decided to turn in and see if they could help. My quick decision to turn and a good bit of sand on the road combined for a slippery environment. As I turned, the bike started to slide, and before I could get my feet down, I was on the pavement. I had pulled the rear brake handle, but of course nothing happened. It wasn't a particularly hard hit, but added to the tire situation, this was a tough afternoon, for sure. I ended up with a few extra scrapes but nothing of consequence. My legs have taken a beating over the years, so a couple of new scars won't matter much.

Thus began the story of yet another angel. Mr. Walker, ATV guy, had desperately wanted to help, but he confirmed that the only way to inflate the tire was with the proper fitting that I had lost. He told me the nearest bike shop was on St. Simon's Island, estimated at 30-40 miles away. I recalled that Kenny Roberts, a friend from home, was vacationing with his family on St. Simon's Island at that very moment. I called Kenny and asked if he would consider stopping at that bike shop, picking up a couple of the fittings and dropping them off to me as he headed back north that evening. Kenny said that he would be glad to, and that I had caught him just before they left the island.

With all that in place, I soon called Kenny with the name of the motel that I found. Within about 45 minutes, Kenny, his wife, daughter and granddaughter pulled in the lot. We talked for a while, with me hoping to treat them all to ice cream. They had plans with Kenny's sister-in-law and needed to be on the road soon. I promised to make their extra effort up to them. Bottom line, with that part I immediately inflated the tire. Otherwise, I would have had no choice but to pedal slowly toward the bike shop the next morning. Had it come down to that, my load in the panniers would have had to be reduced and my speed would have been minimal. Nothing about that long ride would have been fun. Had the tire separated from the rim during the ride, my only hope would have been to fix it without any further damage.

A few comical things happened at the motel. When I stopped to check in, I had already been told that the motel was decent and affordable by the workers at the tire place. I knew what a room would cost and had that confirmed. Nothing about the room was special, but there was nothing wrong with it, either—except for the fact that I was first told that it was a non-smoking room, and yet I found ash trays in it. When I asked one of the owners about that, he told me, "Well, we shouldn't really let you put the bike in the room." What my bike in the room had to do with whether it was a smoking room or not was beyond me. However, they did agree to take the ash trays out of the room because "no one really smokes in it anyway!"

Then, when the Roberts family drove into the parking lot, the owners came out and told them, "Only one in this room! Only one in this room!" They kept checking until the Roberts drove away.

After all is said and done, I was settled down in the motel following 70 miles with way more effort than expected. Thanks to the Roberts family, I was back on track. That was my second flat of this ride, now at about 2,000 miles. Six flats in about 6,100 miles was not bad. With that average, I hoped to have no more tire problems on this trip.

On Saturday morning, I also hoped to start riding and put the experience of the flat tire, the heat and trying day behind me with a better one. Dawn arrived with plenty of optimism that I could have a much better day. My route would be easy to follow because it involved only two main roads. After I left town on Highway 301 and found an almost deserted first 20 miles, a better day did seem possible. Good shoulders and pavement continued as I pedaled into Nahunta. Nahunta is another Georgia town that has several main roads coming together at a junction, with the major businesses being several bustling convenience stores. I stopped at one of them and reloaded my almost empty bags. There was a charity car wash going on with the help of a lot of teenage girls. Girls were posted at all the intersections, obviously having a good time trying to flag down vehicles. They got lots of waves and smiles back, all of it making for an interesting time. Nothing was said about washing my bike, but they did wave to me as I rode away.

Folkston was the next town, with highway rumble strips the only thing marring my light mood. But even the dreaded rumble strips couldn't really cause a problem for me because traffic remained light. I had room to navigate amid the cars, and we all continued on. I had heard that Florida was cyclist friendly and did not use rumble strips, so I hoped this particular set would end at the state line. That is exactly what happened. Once in Florida, the paving improved, and a wide bike lane started immediately.

I was glad to be out of Georgia. The poor roads and logging truck traffic made Georgia a hard state to cycle through. The state does not believe in labeled bike lanes, but it does believe in rumble strips that force the cyclist into the traffic lane. Cyclists should be careful when riding in Georgia. It is great to be in Florida!

Chapter 13
— Northern Florida —

*Traveling the final state with good roads
and bike lanes*

Throughout the planning and actual ride, I had looked forward to my arrival in Florida for several reasons. I often had read about how friendly the state is to cyclists and that most of its roads are in good shape. Over the years, I had traveled to Florida often and had been as far south as Miami in a car. However, nothing beats seeing a state from the bicycle seat, and so many parts of it would still be new to me. No doubt, there would be challenges from time to time as I travelled the ride's longest state, measured from north to south. Challenges at the top of my list were anticipated heavy traffic at times and the heat and humidity of late July and early August, especially as I neared Key West.

When my ride through Georgia ended, I was battling rumble strips and roads that didn't offer quite enough room to ride comfortably. My hope was that the rumble strips would end as soon as I crossed the Florida line, and they did. Never did I see rumble strips again. I crossed over to a smooth ride on nearly new pavement, with generous bike lanes.

Right away, I rediscovered my asphalt friend last seen in New Jersey as I rode onto US 1. The historic highway has many advantages that I have detailed before, but suffice it to say that US 1 usually offers options that are not always available otherwise. Heading the list are plenty of stores to provide the things cyclists need and options on motels.

After reaching Florida, I stopped for the night in Callahan, completing a pleasant ride of 81 total miles. The heat didn't reach predicted temperatures, and a few showers helped cool the road off. I also enjoyed seeing a magnificent lightning show from a distance. In an effort toward full disclosure, I'll note that road kill now consisted of an occasional armadillo or raccoon. From my bicycle, I saw that Florida makes an effort to keep the roads clear of trash and road kill, too.

Callahan was a nice town with an ample supply of stores, such as the Winn-Dixie grocery nearby. We used to have Winn-Dixie stores in North Carolina, but no longer as far as I know. They seem to be thriving in Florida. I got plenty of my favorites at good prices, including lemonade, watermelon, Greek yogurt and bananas. I anticipated getting a good night's sleep and was excited by the prospect of rolling deeper into Florida and seeing some good scenery the next day.

I did get a good sleep but was concerned by the early weather forecasts on Sunday, July 28. They warned of serious heat in the area I would be riding. I took a small chance and left my room to begin the ride while it was still dark. One of the reasons I felt comfortable with a pre-dawn departure was that the map showed a long and straight stretch on A1A for the next 20 miles, and I expected a good bike lane as well. For one of the few times in my north to south trip, I was able to ride directly toward the sunrise, which I've found to be a real treat throughout my cycling experiences. My west to east cross-country ride offered this same opportunity on every clear morning. I found strength and confidence in each and every one of those sunrises, always just shortly after my morning prayers.

After passing through O'Neill and lots of big stores during the early morning, I knew I had arrived in the Amelia Island area because of the big bridge that gave me a panoramic view of the resort landscape. That is about all I saw of Amelia, though, as I turned south and passed through the edges of Fernandina Beach and American Beach.

In this area, an impatient driver told me to get off the road and onto the sidewalk. Then a military truck pulled by me with a wide boat on a trailer. When we reached the next stoplight, there was not enough room for me to ride by the boat without leaning my head over. The passenger rolled down the window to say something, and I pointed to the best sign in Florida. With perfect timing, just in front of us was a "Share the Road" sign. He rolled the window back up. I never had to say a word.

Next up on the road was the impressive Talbot State Park. Here, I enjoyed my first look at the kind of natural beauty I expected of Florida, just after realizing how much the air temperature was warming up. Several things about this park system stood out. The state had taken an old bridge that ran beside the new highway and dedicated it to recreation of several types. Cyclists, runners and fishermen were taking good advantage of the old bridge to enjoy this Sunday morning. By my count, several hundred people were on the bridge. The state park also had a huge parking area with nice restrooms, reminding me once again that Florida seemed to be making a real effort to offer recreational opportunities to its citizens.

Just ahead of the bridge exit, on the ocean side, was a truly amazing sight. I saw hundreds of pelicans, most of them in the trees but many in the water as well. Never had I thought of pelicans as massing in groups, but this seemed to be some sort of pelican convention. People were taking photos of them, so this occurrence may not have been all that common.

After passing through the park, I began a search for the Mayport ferry. It looked close to the park on the map but was in reality several miles away. I pulled into a staging parking lot on my bike and secured a spot before realizing the next ferry was not due for 20 minutes. That was plenty of time to bike back out of the parking lot and get a cold drink and a couple of snacks at a convenience store directly across the road. The temperature had continued to rise, so much that a cold drink felt great. Back at the parking lot, the ferry was pulling in, and the flagman told me to wait until all the cars drove on. I did just that and found a good place to lean my bike during the ferry ride. Evidently the car riders had to pay as they drove on, but no one seemed interested in getting my $1 fee. For one of the few times in my life, I had to chase down someone to get them to take my dollar. By the way, the ferry ride took only about five minutes. Just as we pulled into the channel, a huge ship passed by and provided another photo moment.

When the ferry landed, it was now officially hot, but riding the bike generated some breeze, and I forgot about the steamy temperature. The map called for me to ride through a long series of beaches, namely Atlantic, Neptune, Jacksonville and Ponte Vedra. Although I had envisioned plenty of ocean views, in reality there were very few. Most of the water views were blocked by huge houses or small coastal trees. The huge mansions all were gated, and nearly all the gates were closed. I rode for several miles looking at their driveways, a monotonous view broken only occasionally when I passed a local resident on a beach bicycle.

As often happens on the warm days, I used up water quickly and ran out just past Ponte Vedra. I pedaled on through a long stretch that was part of a wildlife refuge. Totally dry and out of water, I knew there had to be a source of water soon. After noticing some construction on a beach house, I spotted a garden hose, and no vehicles were in sight. That spigot didn't have the best tasting water, but it was wet and filled a need. A few miles later, at the end of the wildlife refuge, a very busy convenience store provided some ice and clean water, along with ice cream. Those things brought me back to life, and I was ready to keep going.

Views of the water and beach now became more frequent as I passed through Villano Beach and headed into St. Augustine, which was founded by the Spanish in 1565 and is commonly known as the nation's oldest city. The day had become about as hot as my earlier ride into Statesboro, Ga. As I rode over the bridge into St. Augustine, I saw one of the sightseeing trollies that carry tourists through the historic town. There was a nice motel called the Cozy Inn near the first intersection. Since I was ready to get off the bike, I pulled into the office area to check it out. The air temperature had risen to 96, but the humidity was high enough to produce a reported heat index of 110, very similar to the Statesboro day. I got a room where I found the air conditioning already working hard.

A quick trip to the nearest Winn-Dixie netted plenty of rehydrating foods. The room was one of the top five for the whole ride, and it made for a pleasant evening. On days like this, eating and drinking went on at a steady pace until bedtime. I was only blocks from some of the historic sights and planned to rise at dawn and do some early sightseeing before leaving town the next morning. Today's ride total was 85 miles, plenty for a warm day. I finally got a much needed shower just before going to bed. Within a minute, I was soundly asleep.

The remaining mileage to Key West was about 515, easy to tell because I had started the last Adventure Cycling map. On Monday morning, I waited until there was enough light to cycle a few blocks to several special sites. I found one of the oldest trees in America, advertised at over 600 years old. I made a few photos of what one resident claimed was the most photographed street in America. The entrance to the Fountain of Youth was closed until later in the morning, so I had to pass it by for this trip. Many years before, at least one of my honeymoons occurred in this area. I am pretty sure it was just one.

I rode through part of the Old Town and took in a few more local spots worth visiting, based on the advice of Steve Buell, whom I met as he was out walking that morning. Buell told me that many of St. Augustine's attractions were now commercialized, but he urged me to at least make the effort to visit some select places before leaving. I found the huge lighthouse not open but still accessible for photos. The St. Augustine Alligator Farm was another favorite of Buell's, but it also was closed and I was not willing to wait two more hours to get in. I did find out that during World War II, the Alligator Farm was a huge attraction for soldiers training in the area. A must-see was the huge Spanish fort Castillo de San Marcos, which guards the bay. I would love to someday spend a whole day just walking around the area with no real agenda. I did get lots of good photos before leaving town, and hope to return to do a stop on my book tour here.

A few miles past St. Augustine, I spotted the signs for another historic Spanish outpost named Fort Matanzas. The National Park Service maintained the site and also offered guided tours. I took time to take the boat ride and tour, well worth it as the fort depicts the life of soldiers stationed here to provide an outpost fort to guard St. Augustine. A small pontoon boat took us across the channel to see the fort and the period furniture, clothes, tools, cannons, etc. that gave insight into the life of the six to seven soldiers who would live there for a month at a time. We were allowed to climb to the top of the fort and spend time in the actual crew and officers' quarters. In the 1700s, the small point of land that the fort sits on was surrounded by water. Eventually, the channel was dredged and the land mass is now much bigger.

Back on the bike, I pedaled south yet again. I rolled through beach towns like Butler, Crescent, Summer Haven and then past Marineland. The view of the ocean was again blocked by dunes, trees and houses for most of this ride, but soon the view improved as A1A became an ocean-front road. Painter's Hill, Beverly and Flagler Beach were more fun to ride through because of the much prettier scenery, probably the best since leaving the coastal areas of North Carolina.

I pedaled toward Ormond Beach, where I planned to spend the night. Mike Wright, a friend from home, had arranged for me to stay with Mike Strauss in Ormond. Strauss is a Jet Blue pilot and Wright's best friend since the days that Strauss lived in Gold Hill, N.C. This was going to be a short day, mileage wise. It was time for one of those. After arriving in Ormond Beach, I called Strauss and told him that I was at the local Walgreen's. Strauss gave me directions and said, "The front door is open. Go on in and make yourself at home." I did just that, and at home is exactly how I felt for the rest of the afternoon and evening.

Strauss put me on a beach bicycle called "the Golden Cruiser," and we rode down to Daytona Beach, site of the original Daytona 500 auto race. The first event was actually run on the nearly flat and very wide beach. I met several of Strauss' friends and enjoyed a pleasant stop at a local bar overlooking the sands. Then we rode the bikes back to his house for some pasta and lots of good discussion about Strauss' life in Florida and as a jet pilot, plus some conversation about my life as well. Thanks to both Mikes for setting up a very enjoyable segment where I could envision life as a beach resident. My total mileage for this day was just 52, but well worth the extra rest.

The beach ride on the cruiser bike was much harder than I expected. I had been riding a top-of-the-line touring bike exclusively for two years. All of this riding had been on paved roads except for a few short stints on hard packed surfaces of other types. Nothing compared to the effort required to ride the much bulkier bike with very wide handlebars while wearing sandals. As I followed Mike Strauss, I was just trying to get the hang of the different bike without falling over. One turn was more than I could negotiate, so I had to back up and do it again. A few times, I slipped in the loose sand. I kept reaching for the brake levers even though there were none. Yet all in all, it was a fun ride. I was glad to get back to my Surly, although most people would have felt awkward riding it for the first time.

I left Ormond the next morning after saying goodbye to Strauss, the perfect host. I even had a chance to wash out my clothes in real machines for the first time in a while. It was good to feel rested, well fed and clean as I headed over the bridge toward Riverside Drive and a pleasant ride past more waterfront homes. Very soon, I had arrived in Daytona, the town. Signs were everywhere pointing the way toward Daytona International Speedway, where the NASCAR auto races are now held.

After riding through several streets, I made my way back on to US 1. Once again, my old friend provided a good shoulder for riding and plenty to look at. Still heading south, I wanted to visit New Smyrna and left US 1 briefly to do that.

New Smyrna was one of the prettiest little waterfront towns that I visited during the entire trip. It had a relaxing atmosphere, and the traffic was so cordial that I thought they must all be cyclists. My route was dotted with rows of historic homes—and one other curious thing. I saw what appeared to be an old fort but was amazed to learn that the locals don't really know what it was. The walls have been preserved beautifully, and could have been part of a fort or even a British mansion. New Smyrna is the second-oldest town in Florida and was a main part of the British efforts at colonization.

Back on US 1, I passed through Edgewater, Oak Hill, Scottsmoor and Mims. The weather included rising heat, building clouds with thunder and lightning, and finally some rain. The storm looked ominous as I rode toward it, making me look for possible shelter in case the bottom fell out. But once again, there was just enough rain to cool things off. No downpour occurred, but for some reason the traffic almost disappeared. I often didn't have a car in sight—a first for my ride in Florida.

For the last couple of days, I had considered some more sightseeing in the Titusville area. The Kennedy Space Center is visible from miles away but reaching it entails traveling almost seven miles over a long causeway. The required ride of nearly 14 miles off my planned route made me pass it by, but I did stop at the United States Astronaut Hall of Fame. The Hall of Fame and the Kennedy Space Center are both part of a tourist package, but I only wanted to take the time for one.

The Hall of Fame didn't have a lot of visitors, and I later found out why. The parking lot was huge, capable of holding hundreds of cars, and a space shuttle is there to catch the eye of anyone considering coming in. I had never seen a space shuttle up close and thought this alone would be worth the visit. I paid for an overpriced ticket and began the tour. The first thing I noticed is that many of the exhibits were not operating or would only be open later, even though I was there in mid-afternoon. The tribute to the astronauts was as good as expected, however, with an early space capsule, flight suits and much more. There was a special room honoring those astronauts who were a part of the Hall of Fame. I walked around and enjoyed seeing the information on how the space program had evolved, but I couldn't get my mind away from the fact that there was no discount in price despite the unavailable exhibits. There was a space simulator, the Mission to Mars, which would have been fun. It was shut down, with no explanation, and that along with the other non-functioning exhibits made for a disappointing visit. But the biggest disappointment was that the space shuttle was not part of the tour. From outside there are ramps leading up to various levels of the craft, but we were not given access. After about an hour, I was back on my bike heading south. As I left, I noticed the obvious signs of neglect, including untrimmed shrubs, grass growing in areas of the parking lot and broken pavement. I was glad I hadn't bought a package ticket to the space center, but left wondering whether it would have been just as lackluster.

Titusville is a busy and happening town. US 1 is being widened and resurfaced, much needed in this area. I rode through Cocoa, the TV home of Major Anthony Nelson and "I Dream of Jeannie." I chose to stop and spend the night after 76 miles for the day. The afternoon had turned out much cooler because of the storms that remained in the area. Some major damage and flooding struck Orlando on the same afternoon. I looked forward to some more beach views over the mid-Florida section of my trip. Key West was now about 388 miles away.

Northern Florida was fun, and I felt completely safe on the bike. I wish all the states would consider similar measures to enhance recreation, wellness and fitness by offering bike lanes as the roads are newly paved. I don't know the statistics, but I have seen wonderful usage of the bike lanes where they are available. Other areas have made huge strides in developing bike trails in various forms. From my point of view, this should be the wave of the future. Let rumble strips be limited to road shoulders that are wide enough to have them without restricting the smooth shoulder for use by cyclists. Don't force the cyclist into the traffic lane where real accidents can occur.

Chapter 14
— Central Florida —

Storming down the Florida coast

Most mornings started with me flipping on the TV to find the nearest weather report. I woke up in Cocoa this morning to exactly the forecast I wanted to hear. The Jacksonville station said a weather front was causing lots of good changes to happen already, and I would see more during the day. A cooler day with much less humidity was on tap, with virtually no chance of rain. It all sounded good, but I wondered if the weather guessers really had it right.

Construction work had continued on the new US 1 widening and paving well into the previous evening. The heavy grading equipment worked until about dark, stopping just in time for me to get ready for much-needed sleep. All the big machines were sitting idle as dawn broke on Wednesday, July 30. I rolled the bike across the road and headed south for the 30th day of this adventure.

After just a couple of miles, I rode onto some of the newest and smoothest paving that I had seen. All black and clean, with fresh lines, the brand new bike lanes seemed to be there especially for me, with no another cyclist in sight. Cocoa changed over to Rockledge, but it was hard to tell where. Melbourne was up next, but I left US 1 and headed toward A1A again. These two highways would now be the key gateways to South Florida. I hardly had to look at my maps anymore. A1A usually ran closer to the beach, and US 1 was just slightly more inland.

I crossed over the Indian River and found the beach town of Indialantic, followed closely by Melbourne Beach. I was surprised that much of the prime beach-front real estate has been set aside for parks, along with grills and snack bars and plenty of parking.

Vendors of all types see the southern half of Florida as off season during the torrid summer months, so prices for tourist-related things are down, and shops and even a few motels are closed until fall. Just more room for me and the locals.

Great views abounded on this morning's ride. I saw that the ocean was almost calm as the prevailing westerly winds pushed toward the beaches. I noticed a few clouds starting to build amid quickly warming temperatures, contrary to the earlier weather forecast. I thought of those famous words, "Virtually no chance of rain today!"

Quite a few cyclists were out today, most of them the casual types. Now with well over 6,000 miles of long-distance riding under my belt, I had begun to lump other cyclists into several groups. One of my running friends from back home, Steve Staley, often labeled the runners who are still stuck on themselves and only their own accomplishments as "heroes." Of course, he meant that in a sarcastic way. I can't help but think of cyclists who are out wearing all the latest gear and always pounding hard, never aware of a wave or willing to return one, as heroes, too. The next group consisted of those who are aware of their surroundings, still making good time, but who want more out of the ride than just pounding the pace the whole time. They take time to look around, to see the things that make a particular day special and are happy with the accomplishments of others as well. I felt all along that I am part of this group. The last group, and probably the most fun, includes those who don't have an agenda and just want to ride a bicycle in the wonderful outdoors. They are usually slow, the ones that other cyclists often zip past. The heroes even put on an extra burst of speed, proving once again that heroes are just a cut above. Or so they think. On most days, I envy the people in the last group.

This morning, just about the time I pedaled through Melbourne Shores, a female cyclist on her racing bike blew by me in a big hurry. Like most guys, I thought, "Gosh, I wonder about her. She sure looked good going by." A few blocks ahead, I had an opportunity to find out just what Sherry Starr was like. She took time away from pushing the pace to stop and pick up a large fishing lure from the side of the road, afraid that it might still have its giant hooks attached. Fortunately the hooks had been cut out, but we both stopped to talk and had a wonderful conversation. Sherry told me about her hobbies and particularly about fishing out of a kayak. Pictures from her phone proved how successful she had been. After talking for a while beside the road, sweating and thinking of water, eventually we rode on. Sherry went ahead to see if she could find a certain local place that offers restrooms and refreshments for cyclists. I saw her again just after she had found it, and we both took a few minutes to refresh before parting again. Sherry was definitely the highlight of the day, but I had to get back to reality and complete the day's ride. Sherry had 40 miles of her own as that day's goal.

A few miles later, I came to another of those Florida recreational treasures. The Sebastian Inlet State Park was one of the prettiest places I had seen, especially from high above on a bridge with the inlet on one side and the ocean on the other. The bridge was high enough to let boats pass underneath and gave me a spectacular panorama. On the protected inlet side of the Indian River, there were families enjoying all kinds of water sports. On the ocean side, more huge homes lined the beach. A few fortunate homeowners had what was advertised as ocean to river access, enjoying the best of both worlds.

Further south was Wabasso Beach and also the first drops of what soon became a steady downpour. "This can't be happening," I thought. I looked for cover and realized there was none, so I just pedaled on in the heavy rain. My raincoat was long gone, probably blown off the bike in Georgia. Lightning raced across the sky, and loud thunder was the only sound I could hear besides the splashing rain. I really missed that lightweight raincoat, perfect for cycling. I hoped that somebody else was enjoying it by then.

I rode over another bridge that gave me a better view of more approaching storms. So much for the forecast of "no chance of rain." This rain was going to last for quite a while, though I didn't mind at all. Rain in hot temperatures is for the most part a pleasant experience, especially with no real wind involved, as was the case on this day. I pulled under the cover of a busy convenience store and joined a few motorists who were waiting out the heavy rain. The lightning strikes were very close, with two of them particularly magnificent as the bolts raced to the ground. Immediately, loud thunder rumbled.

With the weather looking bad for the evening, I decided to find a room. I got a little comic relief when I stopped at one place. Clearly, I had awakened the clerk, who unlocked the door and asked what I wanted. I asked, as I usually do, "How much for one cyclist, for one night, and gone very early?" This guy said $40, a good price. I then asked if his Wi-Fi was good, and his response was classic, "We don't have none of that Wi-Fi." I told him I needed it but also asked to see the room. He said angrily, "If I show you the room, I will have to clean it again." As I turned away and headed back to my bike, the clerk followed me out and offered to show me the room after all. It looked OK, but without the Wi-Fi, I would be at a disadvantage. Careful not to step into the room that might require extra cleaning, I thanked Mr. Cordial and headed on south.

Just for a lark, I stopped at a new Howard Johnson's to see whether I could afford its rooms. The motel had a great rate, with Wi-Fi and everything else I could want to make the room comfortable. The desk clerk was the exact opposite of Mr. Cordial, and I happily paid $10 more per night to get all the amenities. A nearby Publix grocery store added to my happiness, and a short ride in the rain loaded my bags with lots of good things to eat. This was the first Publix where I noticed bagels on sale late in the day for $1 for a six-pack. I took advantage of that several more times on the rest of the trip.

Back in the room, I opened the door to an outdoor sitting area and hung out my wet stuff, hoping it would dry. I didn't have much success, but still enjoyed watching the rain fall gently. My mileage total for today was 64. I went to bed after listening to the weather forecast about a tropical storm possibly threatening southern Florida. By this time, I was more than a day ahead of pace, but I still didn't want to waste any time just sitting out a storm because of high winds.

I woke to more clouds and another rainy forecast. Looks like the improving weather was forgotten. I guess steady rain for 16 hours will do that. The roads were wet when I left, but the traffic was not particularly heavy. I crossed over the Intracoastal Waterway bridge before daylight but felt safe in my excellent bike lane. This bridge was higher than many, with pedestrian walkways and benches making casual recreation even more attractive. As I turned south on A1A, I rode into a headwind. Views of the beaches were mostly blocked, again making the ride a little more boring than expected.

Two unusual sightings helped out somewhat. A huge Florida Power and Light facility had multiple entrances, plenty of huge buildings and lots of clear green water in concrete pools. The National SEAL Museum, as in Navy SEALs, was also along the way that morning. I was interested to see that the museum is not funded by the United States government. I would have liked to visit the museum, but it was too early in the morning for it to be open, so I reluctantly rode on.

I passed through Fort Pierce, then Stuart and Port Salerno. Huge clouds were building behind me again, and rain looked imminent. As I neared Hobe Sound for the first time that day, so did the rain. I waited out yet another downpour for about 30 minutes before heading on. The decision about what route to take played into a series of happenings for the rest of the afternoon. I could have gone left and headed out to the beaches, but I chose to ride straight ahead on US 1 through a long series of hills, unusual for Florida, that looked a lot like sand dunes. I didn't see anything like this in Florida otherwise.

Yet another major cloud bank was forming to the west, complete with more lightning. It looked daunting enough that I called ahead to check on the only motel in Tequesta, the next town. Eventually, I received a call back telling me the motel was full. Apparently, more tourists were in town because it was the week for the two-day lobster "short season" that offers a mini preview of the upcoming regular Florida spiny lobster season, and that may have been why no rooms were available. I remember feeling pretty good that afternoon, despite the uncertainty about finding a room for the night with another storm looming.

I rode into Tequesta, a beautiful tourist area where several celebrities have homes. I heard later that Celine Deon and Alan Jackson have homes there, as does at least one member of the presidential Bush family. I didn't expect to be in Tequesta long and just kept pedaling. I noticed a Publix grocery store and a Wendy's on my right, as well as a black SUV that was waiting to enter the traffic lanes. Then, everything suddenly changed.

As I rode in front of the SUV, the vehicle accelerated straight toward me. I swerved to the left and yelled, "NOOOO!" For a moment, I thought I might avoid the car, but as the front bumper hit my right leg and pushed into me, I knew there was no escape.

Within a split-second, I was lying in the next lane with my bike between me and the car. Worst of all, the SUV was still coming toward me. I distinctly remember its black front bumper looming larger above me as the vehicle drew nearer before finally turning just as I protectively threw up my hands.

I realized the danger had passed, but now I had to assess what possible injuries I had sustained. I was on my back with my feet still pointed toward the bike. As I became more aware of my surroundings, my first thought was to try to sit up. But as I started to move, I heard someone behind me say, "No, stay down. Don't try to get up." Later, I realized it was driver of the car in the adjacent lane. I sat up anyway and said calmly to the lady in the van directly behind the collision: "She just ran over me." The lady said, "Yes, she did. I saw it."

The sirens of the police and fire department were already near. The traffic had stopped all around us. The lady who hit me had parked her SUV partly on the sidewalk and was coming toward me. I had picked up my water bottle and for some reason handed it to her. "I was looking at the storm and didn't see you," the woman said. "Are you hurt? If you will tell them that you aren't hurt, I will buy you a new bike." I told her that all of those things would work out somehow.

About that time, I realized that both my shoes had been knocked off and were near the bike. I picked up the shoes and put them back on, but saw that one sock had a 50-cent-piece-sized hole in it just above the ankle. Both feet were tingling, a fact that would later become more important. Nothing seemed to hurt, but even so, the responding firefighters urged me to go to the hospital. I told them I was OK, and they still insisted that I should have a thorough examination. I looked at my bike about that time and realized it was still in the road. For some reason, it seemed important to get the mangled mess out of the street and over on the sidewalk. I picked the bike up and carried it over there, as well as a few pieces of plastic from the front of the car.

I honestly felt sure that I was not hurt and was more worried about the bike. Within a few days after the accident, I realized that the firefighters were right, and an examination would have been the wisest choice. But my mind was laden with apprehension that this could well be the end of the ride, and I still had no concept of the seriousness of the accident. I could have been slightly dazed. Nothing seemed real at the time.

The firefighters took my blood pressure and pulse, but I never heard the results. The police officers took over and got a statement from one of the witnesses before asking me what had happened. I told the officer that the woman in the SUV drove straight into me. He asked for my license. I gave it to him as he turned his attention to the driver. Three of the firefighters gathered around and asked me again if I was OK. I told them something like, "I think I am, but my bike is not. I still need to get to Key West."

When I had a few seconds alone, I just stared at the bike and looked south. I thought of how far there was to go to finish the ride but struggled to form a concept of just how to do it. The thought never entered my mind to give up the goal. I certainly didn't know much about the area. One thing that did register immediately was that I had built up almost two days of cushion against my already scheduled flight time from Key West to home. At least I could take a day or so to sort this out if need be.

One of the firefighters said, "What are you going to do? Maybe you could stay in the motel down the street and figure out what to do." I told him that the motel was full, and I certainly couldn't ride the bike any more. Captain Dan Tilles said, "OK, why don't you come back to the fire station with us, and we will help you figure it out? We can strap the bike on the back of the fire truck. Is that OK?" It all sounded great to me. They checked with the police officers to see whether I could leave and got the OK.

Peter Allen and Josh Kitzi, the other firefighters, told me on the ride back to the station that they expected to find me seriously hurt or worse when they heard the accident call. Often, when a car hits a cyclist, the rider is knocked into the next lane and run over by an unaware motorist. I was really starting to feel blessed, although the whole incident still seemed to be part of dream. While we unloaded the bike, Peter called the nearest bike shop to tell them what had happened, and Josh got the OK to take me there. We quickly formulated a plan to get a replacement bike, although it might take until the next day. All of the firefighters thought there was a motel back in Hobe Sound, the same place as the nearest full service bike shop.

After a few pictures, Josh and I were on our way to Bike Street in Hobe Sound, marking my second visit there for the day. I walked into their shop, and Dawn and Matt were ready for me. They had picked out a couple of bikes that might work to finish the ride and would hold at least some of my gear. We agreed on a Trek 1000 road bike, and immediately Matt went to work on it. Dawn tried to find me a room for the night, but her only options were back in the wrong direction. The motel in Hobe Sound had recently closed. I thought quietly, "Is there a possibility that I might be able to be on another bike tonight?" Matt continued to work as I made some calls home to let my daughters and editor know what had happened, but also to assure all of them that I was fine.

The time of the accident was just after 3 p.m. By 5:45 p.m., I had my downsized gear mounted on the Trek, and another Bike Street employee gave me a ride back to the scene of the accident. Bike Street agreed to ship the mangled Surly back home, and with a hurried adjustment of the seat height on the Trek, I was ready. I said goodbye to Matt Gebhart and Dawn Arvin, and thanked them for their incredible work. I left with Brian Liles to head back to Tequesta, not sure where I would spend the night or how far I would have to go to find a room. My feet were still tingling, and there were numerous road rash areas that needed some attention. I had not eaten for hours. But more than anything, I needed to ride the bike for some miles before I shut it down that night.

When Brian dropped me off near the accident scene, I had lots of things to think about. I had never ridden a bicycle with the gearing or the shifters that the Trek has. I didn't know where I would spend the night. The Surly was a heavy bike, the Trek was much lighter. Another "Nothing to do but do it" moment.

The Trek bike was certainly a good one, but I was worried how long it would take me to get comfortable with the shifters. The Trek made use of the brake lever to downshift the gearing, while it had a separate little tab near the top of the handlebar to upshift. Dawn had told me at Bike Street that it would take only minutes to get comfortable with that, and I knew it was time to get used to them.

Just after I started pedaling south, a driver in another SUV blew past me and tooted her horn twice, just before sharply turning right into the parking lot of a CVS. She cut me off very abruptly, and I was glad that the Trek had good brakes. This could have been a good thing, because I then knew that the bike would do what I needed it to. Just being on the replacement bike for a few miles eased my mind from the events of the afternoon as I looked toward the remaining miles to Key West.

I pedaled by the accident scene, now completely clear and with much less traffic. I started experimenting with the shifters and began to feel good about that. A quick call to the Hampton Inn in Juno Beach confirmed the distance, price and availability of a room. Andy Atkinson, the desk clerk, was extremely helpful, and I pedaled that way just as the sun went down. A quick stop at another Publix yielded some food for later. Things were improving dramatically.

The best room of the whole trip seemed fitting after what had transpired during the afternoon. That is exactly what I got, and Andy talked with me about my ride and wanted to know how he could find more information. We talked a little about the accident, and Andy wanted to know what he could do to help. I gave him the newspaper website, and within minutes he had it linked to the Hampton Inn website. I made it to the room late but checked in with Andy Mooney, the newspaper's night editor, and told him what had happened. With a sore body, I sat down to eat and write. Just before midnight, I went to bed, although there was not a comfortable position to be found. I planned a late start, hoping to get some needed rest. Sleep was fitful as I thought of the events of the afternoon and the uncertainty of riding the new bike tomorrow. I had completed 69 miles that day, and 256 remained to reach Key

West.

After nearly 73,000 running miles and almost 6,500 on these bike journeys, I had never tangled with a car like this or been in a serious accident. I will always remember Tequesta and all the wonderful people I had met that day. Never had there been a day in my life with so many angels. It is impossible to express the immeasurable appreciation that I have for their efforts. I was blessed today, possibly more than I will ever understand. My prayers that night reflected on those blessings.

Chapter 15
— Southern Florida —

Rolling again: The homestretch into Key West

With my eyes wide open well before my usual starting time, I decided to go ahead and get up. I was sore, and all the places of road rash were stinging and tight, so just about any movement reminded me of yesterday's accident. With such a nice room, I hated to abandon it for the road after only about nine hours. Regardless, I needed to resume the trip and continue to put the events of yesterday behind me. I wanted to make some headway today while becoming more efficient on shifting the Trek 1000.

Andy at the Hampton Inn had let me put the bike in the room, so I rolled it through the door and leaned it against an outside wall. I came back into the room for my usual prayer session, needing to thank God this morning just a little extra for the fact that I was not seriously injured. I felt no pressure at all today, more at peace with myself and the ride than I had been for weeks. I resolved to make today, August 1, a great day.

A good Hampton Inn continental breakfast boosted my energy as I left and walked the bike out toward US 1. Just as I was ready to mount up, I saw the contents of a wallet spread all along the side of the road. The owner was a local female student, so I gathered up all the cash, cards and other things and took them back into the motel. The morning desk clerk gladly took the wallet and promised that she would contact the student. The delay in starting didn't bother me at all, and the result should be well worth the time.

Right away, I was reminded how much lighter and responsive the Trek bike was compared to the Surly. Though the Trek wouldn't have held up to all the abuse and pounding for thousands of miles, it certainly had the ability to carry me the rest of the way to Key West. I had left my sleeping bag and tent with Bike Street so the shop could ship them home along with the damaged Surly. I was now hauling less than 20 pounds of gear on the bike—considerably lighter than the 35 pounds I started with.

For the first couple of hours, I rode by more gated homes. As had been the case on earlier parts of the trip, most had the gates shut tight. Towns on the route were Riviera Beach, Palm Beach, West Palm Beach and South Palm Beach. It was about this time that I got lost and headed away from what looked like the beach frontage road. I stopped to ask a policeman who was setting up a speed trap whether I had made a wrong turn. He assured me that I had not; so on across a bridge I went. I continued to ride until I saw a convenience store and decided to ask again. The clerk told me to turn around and ride back across the bridge, and back past the policeman, and take the first right and I would be on A1A again. The policeman had heavily tinted windows, so I could not see his reaction when I rode back by and pointed the right way. Just as I turned on to A1A, Lake Worth resident Gerard Guarino rode up beside me. Gerard had a lot of experience riding his bicycle in other countries and on long rides in the United States as well. We must have ridden 10 miles together, talking about all kinds of things. We made a couple of photos when Gerard needed to turn off, and I kept heading south. People like Gerard and Sherry Starr made the ride way more fun, especially with their insights into the local area.

Still on A1A, a few minutes later I heard Gerard calling my name. He had forgotten to invite me to breakfast and came back to do it. I knew that the timing just wasn't right, considering that I would have to backtrack quite a ways. So, with some regret, I declined and again shook his hand and headed on. More exclusive homes lined the streets on both sides as I passed beaches like Ocean Ridge, Boynton, Delray, Highland, Boca Raton, Hillsboro and Deerfield. This was another area with the ocean on one side and the river on the other,

124

where most homes had a boat anchored. Plenty of great views were available because I rode so close to the water. It seemed to be a nice day for exercise as well, with lots of cyclists and runners out. Most were friendly and returned my greeting as we passed.

Pompano Beach was coming next, and I began to think about stopping there for the afternoon. Some of the motels had their off-season rates posted, and I thought it would be fun to spend the night this close to a famous beach. I was almost two days ahead of pace and could afford the time. The tropical storm was now deemed to be no threat to South Florida, and with just three more riding days to Key West, stopping in Pompano seemed the right thing to do. I made a few calls about rooms, not really excited about the answers, and decided to stop at a decent looking place a block from the beach. When I talked to the clerk, his price seemed high, so I decided to ride a little longer and take my chances. A couple more blocks riding brought me to the Sea Cove, where I got a great price and a step back in history. The room had a gas kitchen and was very comfortable. The owner let me borrow a beach chair, and within 30 minutes, I had my feet planted in the beach sand. With nothing else close by, my food came from a Walgreen's. Others had the same idea, and the selection was pretty good. I had ice cream twice. Two hours of relaxation on the beach hit the spot, and with only 54 miles for the day, I was ready for an early ride into Miami tomorrow, hoping to make it safely through the big city.

Late in the afternoon, I headed back to the room. It was time to send my daily update to the paper. I slowly walked back to the room and enjoyed the picture perfect afternoon. I reached for the key to the room and couldn't find it. Thinking I had lost it on the beach, I headed back to the same spot and found that a youth lifeguard class had now taken over the area. I felt there was little chance of finding the key and decided to go back to the office and pay for another one. It was embarrassing to stop in and tell them that I had lost my key so quickly. The owner gave me another key and only charged $5 for it. I thought that was very reasonable. Now I could get in the room and finish my work. Just as I got to the room, I realized that the first key was hanging from my T-shirt, just under my chin. All the time that I had been searching for it, the key had been there. That included the time spent telling the owner that I had lost the key. He probably got a good laugh out of this scenario, as did I.

After another restful evening, I headed toward Miami while the sky was still dark. I knew the bike lanes were good, and evidently others did, too. There were hundreds of cyclists of all types out riding. The humidity was thick, and the temperature was warm. As I approached Ft. Lauderdale, the hotels became mega-size, one right after another.

One of the comical occurrences of the trip happened next. It was probably funny to others much more than it was to me. I was supposed to ride by the Ft. Lauderdale/Hollywood International Airport on US 1. A huge group of cyclists was on the same road that morning, but they were all going as fast as they could. Pretty soon they pulled away from me. I saw the airport coming up and thought I was following the right road. Soon I saw the sign for arrivals and departures and realized that I was heading into the airport. Somehow I had to get out of there. The traffic was heavy and fast, and there were no exit opportunities. I finally found a section missing in a concrete wall and walked the bike through it to get back on US 1 again, but this time going north—which, of course, was the wrong way. Just then rain started to fall. I found a pet boarding facility open and got straightened out by walking the bike across the busy highway yet again and paying more attention to the right road the next time. I wasted close to an hour being lost and wet, too.

Just past the airport, I had to find A1A again and head toward Dania Beach. Fortunately that worked out well. I rode past lines of huge hotels in Hollywood and Hallandale. Next up was the entrance into Miami. The hotels got even bigger, but I was more impressed with the drivers and the bike lanes. No problems occurred until the rain got steadier. Some flooding in Miami Beach caused close to a foot of water on at least one street. Drainage must have been poor because the amount of rain didn't warrant all the water in the streets. I headed over toward downtown Miami on Venetian Lane, actually a toll road for cars.

Just past the toll bridge, I found myself in Miami. Traffic was suddenly bumper to bumper, with more flooding in the streets. I was supposed to be on US 1, but I couldn't find a sign for it. I asked several times and finally was told which street would become US 1. Still no signs verified my goal until I rode right onto US 1. This time Interstate 95 was ending, and US 1 was taking the brunt of it. The traffic at this point was worse than in New Jersey. Vehicles drove much too fast, and the horn blowing had returned. One local told me about a bike path underneath an elevated train track and said I should take it to stay safe. After several close calls, I spotted the bike path. For once, I was willing to give it a try. The bike path meandered back and forth and was hard to follow. Sometimes it just ended, and I had to hunt for the next segment. The bike path was intended to connect Miami's metro stations.

I realized soon that this was going to be a long journey to get out of Miami. The numbered streets were well up in the hundreds, something like 132nd Avenue, when I discovered the bike path had become much better. Suddenly there was a road for use only by bicycles and city buses. I found out later that Dade County runs its transit service all the way to the Keys. The bus/bike road ran right beside US 1, so I had no trouble keeping up with where I should be. I planned to spend the night in Homestead and rode the bike path until I was in the town limits.

Once I saw signs indicating I was in Homestead, I figured it was time to make a few calls and see what my room for the night was going to cost. The first two motels I called were in the $80 range, and I decided to keep looking. One of the folks from Salisbury had suggested the Day's Inn, but my luck had not been good with them.

I especially remembered the ripoff desk clerk in New Jersey, but this time I was wrong. I rode into the Homestead Day's Inn and ended up with a great room and breakfast for less than $50. I did ride more than a mile back to the Publix for groceries but easily returned to the room before yet another major thunderstorm hit the area.

Just two days of riding remained, and I was at the gateway to the Florida Keys. I loved the new bike for this short segment. The lighter bike was like a reward for the long ride's home stretch. Tomorrow would be another adventure after today's 74 miles.

I awoke to threatening skies and a similar forecast. Rain seemed to fall daily, and storms with lightning were usually a part of them. Since I'd lost my raincoat, maybe it was time to consider buying one. Today's predictions included heavy rain over the Keys, so it just seemed a matter of time before I would get really drenched.

As soon as I left the Day's Inn, I stopped for some food items at another busy convenience store. People were loading boats and vehicles with all the things they might need for Sunday in the Keys. I left the store and headed south onto US 1, now a freshly paved straight highway with nice bike lanes. Previous warnings of crazy drivers worried me a little, but the early morning traffic was moderate, and virtually none was yet coming out of the Keys. The rain did start and came in waves. I could see numerous storms in the distance. There wasn't much wind, however, and that made the ride manageable.

The first stop was at Key Largo and a visitor center just after 9 a.m. I got some advice on where I might stay and also learned there was a good selection of rain jackets and ponchos at the Kmart. I stopped just long enough to pick out a bright red one. I now had a raincoat and wondered if the rain would soon stop because of it. It was only drizzling anyway, not enough to wear the jacket yet. After a few minutes, the rain stopped, and I never had to use the new raincoat.

I saw signs for crocodile crossings, although it seemed they would have a hard time climbing the black chain-link fences lining both sides of the road. Traffic was building, especially heading north out of the Keys. I passed through small communities like Rock Harbor, Tavernier and Plantation Key. Plenty of big boats and RVs were traveling on both sides of the highway, still not a major concern to me. Showers continued to fall, but I missed the worst of them. It was cool to see all the daytime lightning in the distance.

The good bike lanes ended on occasion, and when they did, I had the option of riding a separate bike path. There was plenty of construction going on, and flooding from recent days left the bike path impassible at times. Once in a while I had to venture out into the traffic to avoid standing water but found that easy enough. Only an occasional rider or two on beach bikes was using the bike lanes or path, so I mostly had them to myself.

Islamorada was the next town, well stocked with good stores and choices of supply. I realized that the issues of being able to get food and water as I needed them were now of little concern. Plenty of groceries and convenience stores were available. Layton and Key Colony Beach were the next small towns as I continued south over numerous bridges and the one main road.

After an easier than expected trip, I stopped in Marathon to find a place to spend the night. Marathon is considered the halfway point of the Keys. Motel prices were some of the highest that I had seen, and I expected this to continue until I left the Keys. After checking a few places, I found an apartment-type room at the Sandpiper Motel that I was happy with. This one included a full kitchen as well and a convenience store nearby. The apartment was decorated colorfully, with lots of plants inside and many more outside.

With more wet weather expected, I had made a food run and returned to my room by late afternoon, just before more rain began to fall. On many of the bridges, I had fought a severe headwind that had nothing to block it. The winds probably came from the storms, so I hoped for better conditions on the last day of riding. Total mileage today was 84, leaving less than 60 to Key West.

With more heavy rain expected for Monday, I thought of possibly spending an extra day in Marathon. My airplane ticket home was not until Thursday, and I already knew that motel rates in the Keys were very high, offseason or not. While planning the trip back in May, I had worked on this with my favorite travel agent, Allison Tuck at Travels by Allison. She was able to make the flight home from Key West count as a round-trip combined with the earlier flight to Bar Harbor. I went to bed planning to decide on Monday morning whether or not to head on to Key West. Rain and more thunder and lightning pounded the area as I fell asleep.

I got up on Monday knowing that despite the forecast, I was going to Key West that day. I looked outside and water was standing everywhere, making it likely that the bike paths would be even more flooded than they were yesterday. The stormy forecast said that heavy rain was falling over Key West that morning, and I could see those clouds far to the south. I pushed the bike outside and went back in for my prayer session before the final day of riding on this trip. The peace of these prayers always comforted me, and today was more of the same. I had survived a serious accident and was now within sight of the end of another epic journey. Today would be a good day!

I made a few photos of the motel and the Turtle Hospital across the road. Floridians were partial to their turtles and treated them well. It was common to see areas roped or taped off where a turtle has been seen nesting. I was excited as I left Marathon at dawn.

For years, I had heard much about the Seven Mile Bridge. In some way, it had even taken on a mystical dimension because riding a bike across seven miles of open water would certainly be an unusual experience. Still, I was dreading more of the headwind as I pedaled onto the bridge at the end of the bike lane. Quite a few runners, walkers and cyclists were on the bridge early. The headwind was not there at all. The old bridge was a little rough, so I had to slow my pace, and I noticed that some others were coming back toward me as well. I soon could see the reason why in the distance.

The old bridge had been cut out, and a chain link fence closed off the end of it. Not a thing had been said about this when I rode onto the bridge, but there was nothing to do but turn around and ride back to the end of the old bridge and go get on the new one. That was an extra six miles that I added to the adventure across the Seven Mile Bridge. The new bridge had a good bike lane, and I cruised on across it, still unsure why I hadn't picked up on the fact that the old bridge was not complete any more. I did hear from Darlene Pritchard of Jacksonville that a huge grant has already been awarded to help stabilize the old structure. I hope they add a good sign saying that through-cyclists should ride the new bridge, and wondered how many other cyclists had made a 13-mile ride trying to cross the Seven Mile Bridge.

I passed more of the Keys, including Big Pine Key, Ramrod Key, Summerland Key and Sugarloaf Key. I stopped at another visitor center in hopes of getting more information on where to spend the night once I made it to Key West. Renee made a few calls and got me a better price than I already had for the "Not Your Average Hotel," so I went ahead and booked the room with her. The NYAH had already been suggested by the staff at Eaton Bikes, from where I would ship my Trek 1000 home.

Shark Key and Boca Chica Key were next but didn't offer much to see except for the takeoffs of four fighter jets at the Naval Air Station. I soon had a choice to make, with US 1 heading into downtown Key West and A1A heading east to the beaches. For today, I chose to see the beaches first and find the southernmost point of the United States, my destination for the last 35 days.

A1A past the beaches is a great way to cruise into Key West. The water was beautiful, but the beaches themselves were different than what I expected. They were short in length, and almost no waves were coming ashore. I passed by a chance to dip the front tire of the replacement bike in the water because I still had my gear loaded on it. There would be time for that symbolic act tomorrow. I wanted to go find the huge buoy that signifies the southernmost point, and it turned out to be an easy task. By riding south, I eventually saw where the traffic was headed, and at the end of the street was the marker. About 50 people were in line to see it and have pictures made, and I joined them. The girl in front of me agreed to take my picture, and she did a great job.

With that done, I looked at my map and found Margaret Street. I headed there for the location of the Eaton Bike Shop and the Not Your Average Hotel. My first ride across Key West went well, especially since most of the traffic seemed to be on foot or on bikes. Despite the rainy forecast, the sun was now out, and the weather was beautiful.

I stopped by the bike shop and told them that I had arrived, but would bring the bike in on Wednesday if that was OK. Micah Lemasters said, "That is fine. I want to talk to you about your ride. We are going to ride part of it in reverse later this year." Always willing to talk running or cycling, we made plans to meet the following day.

My first sight of "Not Your Average Hotel" had me wondering about my choice. It appeared to be an old house with just a front door entrance. I leaned the bike outside near several rental bikes and walked through that front door to find a large reception area and the entrance to about five more buildings, pools and hot tubs. I eventually obtained my temporary lodging, a hostel room with four bunk beds and some other unusual things. The door card that simply had to be waved in front of the door to unlock it tipped me off and showed why nothing was average. No tables or chairs were in the room, so I went back to the desk and asked for a chair. The clerk told me that the hotel had no tables or chairs, instead using a concept called TV beds. I ended up putting my few belongings on the floor and the other beds. There was an individual locker for each occupant, but I didn't put much in mine. The room had one of the best TVs I had seen, but it was not viewable when lying in any of the four beds. I had the whole room to myself and ended up using one bed to sleep in and two others to sit and stow my stuff on.

I got directions to what was supposed to be a grocery store and headed there. The prices were terrible, with some things double what they cost in grocery stores at home. I resolved never to return if possible. Upon exiting the store, I was confronted by a rooster. Surprised, I just walked away from him. He had a chicken and a chick following along. I found out later that roosters and chickens were protected in Key West, with a $500 fine for abusing them. I walked down Duval Street, the gathering spot for some unusual characters, and eventually headed back to my room. Some rain came during the night, but I had never felt a drop all day. I was now safely in my unusual and "not average" room, ready to explore Key West for the next couple of days. I had 59 miles for the day, finishing off a grand total of 2,752 miles from Bar Harbor north to Lubec, Maine, and then the long journey to Key West, Fla.

Chapter 16
— Key West, Florida —

Some downtime allows for plenty of reflection

I woke up on Tuesday, August 5, with nowhere to go. At least I didn't have another town or 80 more miles of riding ahead of me. Several times during the night, I woke up planning to check the clock and see how much longer I could sleep. That happened most nights anyway, but not over and over like it did this particular night. It's hard to let go of a long ride. For 35 days, I had been focused on one singular purpose. Now that the goal had been completed, it was time to move on, but my body didn't want to.

When I completed the cross-country ride last summer, I ended up in Myrtle Beach on exactly the same day, August 4. I slept fine at the motel in Myrtle Beach for two nights, and then came home to a long succession of less than productive nights. There were a few health issues mixed in, but for the most part I awakened several times every night thinking I needed to be pedaling. Over the next few minutes, I would have to convince myself that the ride was indeed over so that sleep would come again.

Now, on the morning of August 5, I did have to complete one major goal so that the Maine to the Keys ride could be officially put to rest. I rode over to Smathers Beach and found Arthur from New Jersey walking along the sidewalk. Arthur was spending the month in Key West, and he was glad to come take my photo while I dipped the front tire of the replacement bike in the ocean. It took two bikes and two sets of tires, but the official ride came to a ceremonial end about 7:30 a.m. on Tuesday morning, August 5. Off Smathers Beach, the waters of the Atlantic Ocean and the Gulf of Mexico come together, so it was the perfect place for the dipping.

In retrospect, I should have taken the front tire off the Surly Long Haul Trucker and slipped it in one of my bags for this very moment. Just the tire itself would have made a great picture. We were all in a hurry on the afternoon of the accident. Had I spent the night locally, I would have thought of taking the tire with me for the rest of the trip. The tire was not the only piece of the bike that I should have saved. I left the worn-out gears at Flythe's Bike Shop in New Bern. The gears would have been a good prop for speaking engagements along with the crumpled bike.

I rode away from the beaches and headed back to the NYAH for breakfast. It was time to go explore Key West and slow the pace down for a few days. I had pedaled across 42 bridges since Miami, had ridden on every one of the past 35 days and was still healing from the accident. My plan included only an easy morning ride aboard the sightseeing trolley, hoping to get some idea of where all the major attractions were. The whole island was just two miles by four miles, and I figured that I could walk anywhere I needed to once I knew where I wanted to go.

The trolley was a good deal, with a "hop on, hop-off" policy that allows sightseers to explore at their own pace. I learned lots of unique facts about Key West as the day got warmer. Some of the highlights were the Ernest Hemingway house, the lighthouse, the three Civil War forts and the beaches. I went to the Hemingway house first, hoping the tour of the iconic author's former residence would be interesting. They let me in for half price because of the bicycle ride, and the tour was wonderful. My tour guide was funny, making lots of jokes about Hemingway and his four wives while telling the history of the house.

The lighthouse was just across the street, and I enjoyed a great view from the top of it. Three Union Army Civil War forts in the southernmost town that was never attacked made for some good conversation. The architecture of the historic town was amazing, particularly how the houses were built to make the intense summer heat more bearable.

I heard from Rowan County's Linda Agner, who was vacationing in Key West with her family. She came to see me with her daughter, Sara Agner Maloney, and her daughter-in-law, Ashley Agner. We had a nice visit before they left to rejoin the men of the family.

The Truman White House drew lots of attention from the tour guides. President Truman was a regular visitor to Key West, as were Presidents Eisenhour, Kennedy and Clinton. I walked around the parts of the Truman White House that didn't require an admission fee, with one unexpected delay when I couldn't get the bathroom door open from inside. After much pulling and pushing, it finally opened, but I never figured out why the door decided to stick. The door kept me trapped long enough to make sure I was sweating pretty well by the time I finally escaped.

Key West once briefly seceded from the United States on April 23, 1982. The Conch Republic has been celebrated every year since. The beaches have no sand of their own, and most of it is brought in from the Bahamas. They also have virtually no waves because of the offshore reefs.

In my opinion, the most unusual thing about Key West is the odd treatment of roosters and chickens. Free-roaming roosters and chickens are everywhere, and there is that $500 fine for harassing them. However, recent high poultry numbers have caused some residents to cry "fowl" and work to get the population under control. I could understand why after experiencing my own game of chicken.

I had heard about the street performers and the spectacular sunsets at Mallory Square, so I planned to check out those things. Micah LeMasters from Eaton Bikes and I got together so I could give him some information on what he could expect when riding north from Key West to Charleston, S.C., this fall. Micah lives on a boat in the harbor with his brother, and he told me about some other good places to see the famous sunsets.

A short walk from the harbor took me over to Mallory Square.

That night, the sun hid behind colorful clouds as it set. I was impressed, as were probably a few thousand other tourists. The street performers were good too. I decided to return again the next night for more of the same, hoping for an even better sunset.

Just a few blocks away was Duval Street, the center of the "just about anything goes" philosophy of Key West. I got propositioned on the second night by someone who at least looked like a woman. My main reason to walk down Duval Street was to see the crazy things and to stop at the Walgreens before heading back to the room. Food and snacks were way cheaper in the Walgreens than anywhere else In Key West. The store kept three cash registers running hard to keep up with the demand. Pompano Beach also had a Walgreens with ample food choices near my motel. I saw people at both places making large purchases that included things like frozen pizza. Both Walgreens had good prices on some of my favorite flavors and brands of ice cream.

Wednesday morning, my last full day in Key West, was the best day to visit Fort Taylor State Park. Fort Taylor is the largest of the Civil War forts on the island, and it is very well maintained. A large section of a vintage Civil War cannon remains in the fort, even after its use as late as World War ll to protect the coastal area. The beach in the park was the best on the island, and it was well worth the small fee to use that beach until sunset if desired. I spent much of the morning on the beach after touring the fort. The park staff was obviously doing a good job, even sweeping and raking underneath dozens of picnic tables. The onsite grill was also top-notch. No wonder this was the favorite beach for the locals, according to one of the sightseeing tour guides.

Another time around on the sightseeing trolley gave me the insights of another driver, this one an expert at hunting the iguanas on the island. The large lizards were numerous, making me think the island might not be my favorite camping site.

In the afternoon, I dropped off my replacement bike at Eaton

Bikes to have it shipped back home. Micah allowed me to put most of my remaining gear in the shipping box as well. Late in the day, I headed for Mallory Square and more sunset watching. The sky was clear for this last sunset, and just as the last vivid sliver of it passed below the horizon, the huge crowd cheered. One more walk down Duval and a last visit to Walgreens, and I was ready to head home very early the next morning.

I slept about four hours before rising at 3:30 a.m. to walk to the Key West airport for a 6:20 a.m. flight. The temperature hovered around 83 degrees at 5 in the morning with oppressive humidity. No breeze stirred as I sweated through my shirt on the three-plus mile walk. I looked forward to heading home, and the flights to Miami and Charlotte were perfect. My daughter, Amber, picked me up at the airport for the ride home, and the complete adventure was behind me.

I looked back on this summer's ride, thinking of the challenges I expected. I knew that traveling up north would involve some hilly riding, but it was more challenging than I had anticipated. Much of the northeast, including Maine, New Hampshire and Connecticut, involved constant up and down riding. My Surly bike had climbed to past 11,500 feet last summer in Colorado, but I think it worked harder this summer in the repetitive hills. Proof of this came when the big gears had to be replaced in New Bern, N.C., so that there would be enough teeth to maintain chain contact and finish the ride.

Traffic was also challenging, but not more than I expected. When initially planning the trip, I didn't intend to pass through New York City but did plan to pedal through Washington, D.C., and Miami. The opportunity to ride a bike in New York City was just too good to pass up. None of the big city traffic was terrible, except for the short stretch leaving Miami. Flooding probably made that area much worse than it would have been otherwise.

I'm sure that if I lived in one of the big cities I would learn to love riding in them. Running has always been fun in every major city that I have visited. There certainly have been plenty of resident cyclists in each of the major cities, and they appear to travel with relative ease.

The weather never gave me a hard time. I've said plenty of times that I like riding in the rain providing there isn't much wind. Only on a few bridges did the wind become a factor. The maximum temperature never went over 100, and the lowest temperature was somewhere in the mid-50s. All of this was made for very tranquil traveling compared to last year's extremes.

I envisioned a huge expense for motels and spending lots of nights in campgrounds to keep the costs down. Only once did I pay near $100 for a room, and my lowest was $32.95. That $32.95 was in my top 10 motels of the 35-day trip. Most rooms were in the $40-$45 range. US 1 provided a steady diet of reasonably priced rooms, most of them former mom-and-pop places. Usually, if I didn't have a place lined up, residents gave me top-notch information on where to go. There were a limited number of campgrounds available and only one hostel that I remember. In contrast to my cross-country ride, I never saw a church advertising that it would allow cyclists to spend the night. Those church lodgings were some of my best nights on the cross-country trip. I always slept very well in those surroundings.

Mechanically, I had to use two bikes, and both did well. In retrospect, the Surly did just what I knew it would do. The reliable bike did a great job of carrying my tools, clothes, food and much more while absorbing the pounding of potholes, old pavement and the stress of all the climbing. Swapping out the gear parts in New Bern and flat tires in Exeter, N.H., and near Jesup, Ga., were a reasonable and expected part of this type of riding. The Trek 1000 that carried me through the last 256 miles did the job as well, and I plan to keep it. It was so much fun to ride the lighter bike for that short period. I also plan to use it on some of the shorter endurance rides I have planned for the fall and winter this year.

I knew that my bags, the two Ortlieb panniers and the Trek handlebar bag, would be perfect for my needs. One of the panniers was punctured in the accident, so it will get replaced later. The same rack worked fine on both bikes. The handlebar bag doesn't fit on the replacement Trek, at least not yet. But because it is so handy we will find a way to rig it up.

My tools were perfect again, but I knew from experience that they would be. The CO2 cartridge inflator, Allen wrenches and tire-changing tools were the only ones I had to use. The only glitch was the missing valve stem inflator that Kenny Roberts picked up for me in Georgia. From now on, I will have more than one and keep them in different places in my bags. The small emergency pump worked the only time that I needed it.

Clothing was just about perfect again. The one pair of cycling shorts got washed nearly every night, and I swapped out three Dri-FIT short-sleeve shirts. One long-sleeve Dri-FIT took the chill off the cooler mornings in Maine. I can't remember wearing the long-sleeve wool shirt, but I will still take it on the next ride. The Dri-FIT shorts were perfect when I wanted to wear something with pockets. Several pairs of socks and underwear closed out the inventory of clothing in my bags. I did buy a pair of Walgreens sandals that are now part of my equipment list.

I didn't come home with my favorite rain jacket, but I will get another Tyvek jacket before I ride again. If the next one comes with pockets, that will be an appreciated plus.

Once again, I wore a brightly colored pair of running shoes while riding, and I am glad I did. If I had been clipped into the pedals during the accident, the aftermath might not have been as fortunate. My helmet was a basic model, but it was comfortable and just right for the ride.

My equipment list was also perfect, and I can't think of a change needed. If anything, I may audition a slightly larger tire pump.

For a more detailed list of equipment, see my first book. Nothing changed.

Total cost of the trip came in at just under $3,500, including rooms, flights, food, bike repairs and basic daily needs. That does not include the cost of the replacement bike or the original cost of the Surly or any of the equipment. Bottom line, for just under $100 dollars a day, I got one of my two best vacations ever. Someone reminded me the other day that I would have had to eat even if I had been home, so the only additional expense is the extra food consumption that was directly related to the excessive physical exertion while on the bike.

Concerning food, I have to admit that I love eating 7,000 calories a day. What I don't love is that my strict diet went out the door once again. Yogurt and fruits, especially watermelon, often gave way to my craving for ice cream. Mountain Dew was my caffeine of choice when needed, along with the energy boost of Reese's Cups. I ate too many heated cinnamon buns and other pastries, but somehow all of this fuel worked to keep the legs pedaling.

Sleep came easily. Only on a couple of nights did I have trouble getting much-needed rest. My biggest problem was not getting to bed soon enough. Most of the time, I fell asleep almost as soon as my head hit the pillow. Averaging nearly 80 miles a day on a bike will do that for you.

The scenery was not as spectacular as I had hoped. But then my only measure was the western states of Montana, Idaho, Oregon and Wyoming. Maine, Pennsylvania, Virginia and Florida offered the best views on this ride, and the one magical day on Highway 23 in Pennsylvania was the best of all. In that one day, I saw Revolutionary War and Civil War-era homes and other history; plus, I enjoyed a very basic tour of the Amish farmland.

With all of that said, I have no better reason to make these rides than to meet the people along the way. One of my longtime goals has been to meet at least one new person a day. That average went way up during the 35 days of this adventure. I won't try to list everyone, but I do want to mention a few people one last time in this book. George Pickel, the Bronx PE teacher, made my day when he waited to lead me across the Bronx, but it was our conversation about him being an obese child that really stuck with me. Then there was the wonderful effort that Alex Yu made to help me find a reasonable room on that trying night in North Bergen, N.J. Just the good advice would have been enough, but Yu followed my progress and made sure I was OK. Would I have thought to do that much? I can only hope so, but Alex never hesitated.

Of course, I will never forget the accident in Tequesta. What I'll remember most, however, was the extraordinary concern and assistance from Peter Allen, Dan Tilles, and Josh Kitzi at the fire department and Dawn Arvin and Matt Gebhart at Bike Street. Andy Atkinson helped me make peace with it all when I checked into the Hampton Inn. All of this on a day when I realized how blessed I was, even though the accident had left me somewhat bewildered by a totaled bike and the possible premature end of the ride.

There were many more helpful, friendly people, like the crews at Exeter Cycles and Flythe's Bike Shop. People like Gerard Guarino, Sherry Starr, Bret Ericson and Katie, all good folks that I would love to have as neighbors. So many people helped me with directions or kind suggestions. Thank you all so much for your huge part in making this ride a success.

Finally, the physical challenges of a ride like this can take a toll on the body, as evidenced by the aftermath of last summer's ride. I am glad to say that all medical tests have supported the fact that I came home in good shape this time. The bruising and road rash, and some lingering swelling of my battered feet, all abated in the weeks following the accident. Running has been good, improving daily as soon as I came home. I feel great and look forward to another great adventure, hoping that the next one is not too far in the future.

David Freeze dips the front tire in the bay at Lubec, Maine, easternmost town in the United States.

The granite marker signifying the easternmost point in the US at West Quoddy Head State Park, near Lubec, Maine.

Officer Terry Goan pulled David Freeze over for riding on a four-mile section of US 1.

These guys got David back on the road after a flat tire and brake issue in Exeter, New Hampshire. Left to right: Devan Harris, Billy Hagerty, David Freeze and John Gromek.

George Pickel is a physical education teacher in the Bronx, New York. George rode with Freeze to make sure he found his way across New York City.

Replicas of the winter quarters for George Washington's Continental Army at Valley Forge.

An example of the bike paths in the Maryland/Washington, DC area.

The Sunken Road in Fredricksburg, site of the 18,000 Civil War casualties in December, 1862.

The long three-mile bridge over the Albemarle Sound near Plymouth, North Carolina

The Palmer-Marsh house in Bath, NC is one of the oldest houses in North Carolina, built in 1744.

The free ferry to Aurora, NC.

Freeze pedaled all day to get to Flythe's Bike Shop where Shawn McGuire, Mac Flythe and Steve Mercer stayed late on a Saturday to replace his main drive gears. They were worn out from all the climbing in the northeast.

Freeze saw a small sign that pointed the way Walterboro Air Field and the home of the famous Tuskegee Airmen.

Kenny Roberts and family from Salisbury drove 45 minutes out of their way to bring Freeze a special bike part to Jesup, Georgia.

This oak tree is over 600 years old in St. Augustine, Florida.

Fort Matanzas, an old Spanish fort guarding the river entrance to St. Augustine.

Don't go to the Astronaut Hall of Fame expecting to get inside this space shuttle.

Sherry Starr stopped to pick up a fishing lure lying in the road and started a nice conversation in Melbourne Shores, Florida.

The accident scene in Tequesta, Florida. Freeze's bike was totaled.

Freeze's Surly Long Haul Trucker is no longer usable after it was run over by a motorist in the accident in Tequesta, Florida.

Left to right: Firefighters Peter Allen, Dan Tilles and Josh Kitzi took Freeze back to the fire station, then on to the bike shop and helped make sure that he could get a replacement bike and continue the ride.

Freeze got this Trek 1000 from Bike Street in Hobe Sound, Florida. This was the bike used for the last 256 miles.

153

SECONDFRONT

Monday, July 28, 2014 **3A**

news@salisburypost.com

salisburypost.com

Pedaling through Florida on the hottest day of the trip

The weather experts for the southern Georgia and northern Florida area were calling for serious heat. I left my room in Callahan earlier than people could see me this morning because I needed to only make one turn and I would have a 20-mile straight road with my own bike lane.

I got a photo of my first eastbound sunrise of this trip.

David Freeze

Most of the time I have been heading south. My first road was A1A, and the town of Yulee was first. Lots of big stores were along the road, but they quickly went away. I never knew when I was in O'Neill, the next town.

It was easy to tell when I arrived at Amelia Island because of the huge bridge that signaled entrance into the area. The view off the bridge was about all I saw of it though, as we turned south again. Passing through the edge of Fernan-

See **Freeze**, 4A

DAVID FREEZE / FOR THE SALISBURY POST

The bridge to the left is the live one, as you can see by the bike lane. The bridge on the right is now a state park for biking, walking, running and fishing.

Freeze's column ran daily in his hometown newspaper, the *Salisbury Post*.

Early morning on Fort Lauderdale Beach, Florida.

154

The new Seven Mile Bridge ahead with the old bridge on the right. This is just south of Marathon, Florida.

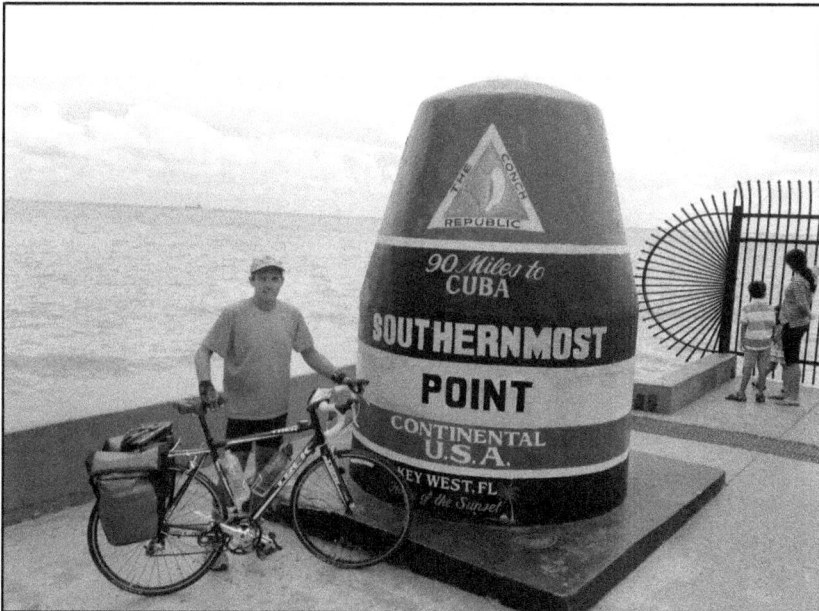

Key West is the southernmost city in the United States. This is the official marker.

The official front tire dipping to signify the end of the ride. The Atlantic Ocean and the Gulf of Mexico come together at Key West.

Sunset in Key West.

156

Epilogue
— Glad for a safe return —

Some downtime allows for plenty of reflection

With this, my second long-distance ride complete and now safely back home, I know that my thirst for great adventure has been only partially quenched. This ride gave me a new perspective on the East Coast of this grand United States of America. We hear often about how America is not the same as it used to be, how things at home and in the rest of the world are falling apart. My long-distance bike rides contradict such statements, and my faith in the people of our nation has never been stronger.

Visiting Maine for the first time got the trip off to a wonderful start, especially starting in Bar Harbor and riding to the eastern-most point of the United States at Lubec. It took me a few days to recover from those initial back-to-back 100-mile days, but those long rides "needed doing," as I often say. Maine set the tone for a scenic and historical ride, just as I hoped it would.

New Hampshire and Connecticut were more physically challenging than I expected. My main gears and pedals eventually had to be replaced after all the constant climbing. I believe that the physical exertion on this ride was at least equal to, and often exceeded, that of my cross-country ride in the summer of 2013.

I began to break the ride up into segments, with the northeastern states being the most physically challenging, both for me and the bike. Next came the major traffic segment, including New York, New Jersey and even part of Pennsylvania. There was seldom a time to let my mind wander, needing to stay alert at all times to think ahead of such a constant vehicle overload. This segment also was the most mentally challenging portion of the ride.

The rest of Pennsylvania, Maryland, Virginia and North Carolina combined for the historical segment. I was exposed to so many great little towns, the Revolutionary and Civil wars, and the Amish farmland.

South Carolina and Georgia took me away from the coast and onto endless country roads. On occasion, I had the chance to lower my alert status but only if the paving was good. I called this segment the "bumpiest and most bone jarring" for the lack of really good roads. Logging trucks kept me on my toes.

Florida, the longest state by far, was a true joy until the accident. I have passed through only one other state that is so friendly to cyclists, especially with all the bike paths, bike lanes and good pavement. Oregon was very similar during the previous summer's ride. Both of them are fine examples of states providing for safe and enjoyable recreation. Still, with that said, my worst accident ever was in Florida.

Reaching the southernmost point of the United States was a big thrill of its own. There was always a long line of tourists waiting to get photos made with the famous buoy.

All my rides come down to people first and scenery second. This summer, I met George Pickel from the Bronx who decided that he wanted to help another cyclist find his way across New York City. Gerard Guarino of Lake Worth, Fla., rode alongside while telling about how to get through Miami, and then turned back toward home before returning to invite me breakfast because he had forgotten to do it earlier.

The firefighters and the bike shop staff will forever be a part of my memory of the Tequesta accident and will hold a special place in my heart. Alex Yu went way beyond in making sure that I was safe for the night in North Bergen, N.J. Kenny Roberts drove far out of his way to bring me a bicycle part that I needed from St. Simons, Ga.

I spent some quality time with Micah Lemasters at Eaton Bikes in Key West as he helped get my replacement bike shipped back home, and I gave him insight into what his own ride to Charleston would be like this fall. Every time I needed help, someone stepped forward—and always they offered their assistance with a smile.

What I will call the Atlantic Coast journey didn't fail to meet my high level of expectation. Overall, this ride was mentally harder than the much longer ride across America. But that is OK; I expected it to be. New York City, Washington, D.C., Richmond and Miami are a part of the East Coast, and I am glad to have experienced them on a bike. The little seaport towns of the northeast, the jungle sounds of riding in the deep Keys, iguana sightings and even all of the crazy motel happenings—it was just too much fun!

Considering what happened medically last year, it was important for me to finish without any long-lasting issues. The doctors checked out any possible damage from the accident, and I have been given a clean bill of health. My running has returned to pre-ride quality without issue. My energy level is fantastic, and I feel great.

"What will be next?" is the question I am asked most often. I'm exploring several shorter rides for the next few months and looking hard at a north-to-south ride in the middle of the country for next summer. What better way to see, hear, feel and smell what can't be experienced any other way?

What would all of this mean without the constant support from so many of my friends and neighbors, as well as all those I have never met from other parts of the country? Not nearly as much. This ride is for you, too, and I am grateful for every single person who follows my rides. There is more to see and much more to do. We'll get after it soon.

www.ingramcontent.com/pod-product-compliance
Lightning Source LLC
LaVergne TN
LVHW051637080426
835511LV00016B/2369